BESONDERE LEISTUNGSFESTSTELLUNG 2007

Englisch 10. Klasse

Aufgaben mit Lösungen
Gymnasium
Thüringen
2003–2006

STARK

ISBN-13: 978-3-89449-652-4
ISBN-10: 3-89449-652-5

© 2004 by Stark Verlagsgesellschaft mbH & Co. KG
D-85318 Freising · Postfach 1852 · Tel. (0 81 61) 1790
5. ergänzte Auflage 2006
Nachdruck verboten!

Inhalt

Hinweise zur Besonderen Leistungsfeststellung

Übungsaufgaben im Stil der Besonderen Leistungsfeststellung

Aufgabe 1:	England in the year 1066 (I)	1
Aufgabe 2:	England in the year 1066 (II)	10
Aufgabe 3:	Teenage moods	19
Aufgabe 4:	Illegal drugs	30
Aufgabe 5:	Bokanovsky's Process – a 1932 fiction of cloning?	43
Aufgabe 6:	Tahoe Extreme Sports Camp – Go Extreme All Day!	54

Aufgaben der Besonderen Leistungsfeststellung

Besondere Leistungsfeststellung 2003

Aufgabe 1:	Young drivers live dangerously	2003-1
Aufgabe 2:	Slamming with Dirk Nowitzki	2003-13

Besondere Leistungsfeststellung 2004

Aufgabe 1:	Branded like Beckham	2004-1
Aufgabe 2:	Shark numbers 'at point of no return'	2004-12

Besondere Leistungsfeststellung 2005

Aufgabe 1:	Around the world in 175 days	2005-1
Aufgabe 2:	Optimistic, responsible and political: the face of today's teens	2005-10

Besondere Leistungsfeststellung 2006

Aufgabe 1:	The world loves SpongeBob SquarePants	2006-1
Aufgabe 2:	Exploring Britain	2006-11

Jeweils im Herbst erscheinen die neuen Ausgaben
der Besonderen Leistungsfeststellung mit Lösungen.

Autorin:

Beatrix Kaufhold

Vorwort

Liebe Schülerin, lieber Schüler,

dieses Buch hilft Ihnen dabei, sich mit den Anforderungen der Besonderen Leistungs-feststellung vertraut zu machen und sich **gezielt auf den mittleren Schulabschluss vorzubereiten.**

Im ersten Teil des Buches finden Sie **Übungsaufgaben** im Stil der Besonderen Leis-tungsfeststellung mit **Lösungsvorschlägen.** So können Sie die Verarbeitung und Darstellung von Informationen sowie die Textproduktion einüben. Die Übungsauf-gaben decken thematisch ein breites Spektrum ab und basieren auf dem gültigen Lehr-plan. Anhand von **Tipps zum Lösungsansatz** erlernen Sie Strategien zur Bearbeitung der Aufgaben. Die **themenspezifischen Wortschatzlisten** können Sie dazu nutzen, sich vielseitig verwendbares Vokabular anzueignen.

Im zweiten Teil des Buches finden Sie die Aufgaben früherer Jahrgänge der **Beson-deren Leistungsfeststellung** mit Lösungsvorschlägen. Diese Sammlung wird jedes Jahr um die jeweils aktuellen Aufgaben erweitert und dient Ihnen als Gradmesser Ihres selbstständigen Lernerfolgs. Wenn Sie diese Aufgaben erfolgreich bearbeitet haben, können Sie stolz auf Ihren Lernzuwachs sein und gehen gut vorbereitet in die Besondere Leistungsfeststellung.

"If at first you don't succeed, try, try again." – In diesem Sinne viel Erfolg bei der Erlangung Ihres mittleren Schulabschlusses!

Beatrix Kaufhold

Hinweise

Die Besondere Leistungsfeststellung

Die Teilnahme an der schriftlichen Besonderen Leistungsfeststellung in der Klassenstufe 10 ist obligatorisch für alle Schülerinnen und Schüler an Thüringer Gymnasien. Die Aufgaben für die Fächer Deutsch, die Fremdsprachen und Mathematik werden durch das Thüringer Kultusministeriums zentral erstellt. Zusätzlich kann auf Verlangen des Schülers nach Bekanntgabe der Noten der schriftlichen Leistungsfeststellung eine mündliche Leistungsfeststellung durchgeführt werden.

Mit der erfolgreichen Teilnahme an der Besonderen Leistungsfeststellung und dem Erfüllen der Versetzungsbestimmungen wird dem Schüler am Gymnasium eine dem Realschulabschluss gleichwertige Schulbildung bescheinigt.

Erfolgreiche Teilnahme an der Besonderen Leistungsfeststellung

Der Schüler hat erfolgreich an der Besonderen Leistungsfeststellung teilgenommen, wenn er die Bestimmungen zur Versetzung nach der Thüringer Schulordnung erfüllt hat. Das bedeutet im Einzelnen:

- Er hat in allen vier Fächern der Besonderen Leistungsfeststellung mindestens die Note 4 (ausreichend) erhalten **oder**
- in höchstens einem Fach die Note 5 (mangelhaft) bekommen und in den anderen drei Fächern nicht schlechter als mit der Note 4 (ausreichend) abgeschlossen **oder**
- in höchstens zwei Fächern die Note 5 (mangelhaft) erhalten, kann diese beiden Noten aber ausgleichen und hat im Übrigen nicht schlechter als mit der Note 4 (ausreichend) abgeschlossen **oder**
- in höchstens einem Fach die Note 6 (ungenügend) erhalten, kann diese aber ausgleichen und hat in den übrigen Fächern nicht schlechter als mit der Note 4 (ausreichend) abgeschlossen.

Ein Ausgleich für die Besondere Leistungsfeststellung ist

- für je eine Note 5 (mangelhaft) durch eine Note 2 (gut) **oder** durch eine Note 1 (sehr gut),
- für eine Note 6 (ungenügend) durch zwei Noten 2 (gut) **oder** durch eine Note 1 (sehr gut)

gegeben.

Erreicht ein Schüler in der schriftlichen Leistungsfeststellung nicht sofort diese Ergebnisse, so ist ein Bestehen nur über die zusätzliche mündliche Leistungsfeststellung in diesen Fächern möglich. Findet damit auf Wunsch des Schülers in den Fächern der Besonderen Leistungsfeststellung eine mündliche Leistungsfeststellung statt, gehen das Ergebnis der schriftlichen und das Ergebnis der mündlichen Leistungsfeststellung im Verhältnis 2 : 1 in die Gesamtnote der Besonderen Leistungsfeststellung in diesem Fach ein. Die nach den mündlichen Leistungsfeststellungen erreichten Gesamtnoten müssen dann die Kriterien der Versetzungsbestimmungen erfüllen.

Bei der Ermittlung der Note für das Schuljahr werden in den Fächern der Besonderen Leistungsfeststellung das Ergebnis der gesamten im laufenden Schuljahr erbrachten Leistungen (Jahresfortgangsnote) und das Ergebnis der Leistungsfeststellung gleich gewichtet.

In den Fächern außerhalb der Besonderen Leistungsfeststellung gelten die Jahresfortgangsnoten als Noten für das Zeugnis. In den Fächern der Besonderen Leistungsfeststellung werden im zweiten Schulhalbjahr der Klassenstufe 10 keine Klassenarbeiten geschrieben.

Die Besondere Leistungsfeststellung im Fach Englisch

Die Besondere Leistungsfeststellung im Fach Englisch setzt sich aus folgenden Komplexen zusammen:

Working on the text und **Creative writing**.

Die Arbeitszeit beträgt 120 Minuten. Als Hilfsmittel ist das einsprachige Wörterbuch Englisch zugelassen. Es stehen zwei Aufgaben zur Wahl, von denen eine zur Bearbeitung kommt.

Der Teil *Working on the text* ist auf das Erfassen, Verarbeiten und Darstellen von Informationen aus dem/den vorgegebenen Text/en gerichtet. Der Teil *Creative writing* erfordert schwerpunktmäßig das Darlegen zusammenhängender Sachverhalte, wobei Sie zwei Aufgabenstellungen zur Wahl haben.

Übungsaufgaben

**Besondere Leistungsfeststellung Thüringen 10. Klasse Englisch
Übungsaufgabe 1**

At the beginning of the year 1066

Edward the Confessor, King of England, is 61 years old, childless and very sick. When he dies on January 5, there is no direct heir to
5 the English throne. Moreover, Edward has not proclaimed any successor to the throne, which causes trouble as three men claim the English crown: Harold Godwinson,
10 Harold Hardrada and William of Normandy all consider themselves to be the rightful successor.

Harold Godwinson, Earl of Wessex, is the most powerful man in England, for Wessex is the richest and most important area at this time. He is a brave and
15 respected leader and the favourite of many English Thanes. He is Edward's brother-in-law and swears that Edward promised him the crown on his deathbed.

Harold Hardrada (also known as Harold III), the powerful Viking King of Norway, claims that his father and his descendants had been promised the English throne by King Hardicanute in 1042.

20 Duke William of Normandy, whose family often supported Edward in the past, is a son of Edward's first cousin and therefore the closest blood relation to the late king.

A few hours after Edward's death, Harold Godwinson manages to get the approval of the Witan and is crowned King Harold II the following day, on January 6.

25 Yet, Harold Hardrada openly refuses to recognize Godwinson as the new English monarch and sends him a message:

Harold the Third, King of Norway, to the honourable Harold Godwinson, Earl of Wessex, greeting. We recommend Us to you and hope this letter finds you safe and sound.

Honesty is the best policy and We kindly would like to remind you of the promise King Hardicanute once made to King Magnus.

You will understand that We are unable to accept your reign over England. It is Us, Harold III, to whom the rightful claim to the English throne has been handed down. Therefore, We wish you to reconsider your accession to the throne and to hand over the English crown to Us.

If you do not wish to follow Our Royal advice, may justice flow like a river and righteousness like a stream that never runs dry.

Awaiting your bulletin of resignation by return of messenger.

With kind salutes
Harold III

Written the Twenty-eighth day of January in the Year One Thousand and Sixty-Six and in the Nineteenth Year of Our Reign.

A Working on the text:
   Reading comprehension and organizing information (25 BE)

1. Show the conflict caused by King Edward's death in a brief and well-organized way.

2. Briefly name the arguments of the different claimants in favour of their succession to the English throne.

B Creative writing (25 BE)

Complete King Harold II's letter of reply to Harold III, King of Norway.

Harold the Second, by the Grace of God, King of England, to His Majesty, Harold the Third, illustrious King of Norway, greeting. We recommend Us to you and hope Our reply finds you in good health.

Pride goes before a fall ...

Tipps zum Lösungsansatz

A Working on the text

1. – Zum Inhalt:
   - Formulierung des Konflikts nach König Edwards Tod
   - Verweis auf die Ursachen dieses Konflikts
   - Nennung der sich daraus ergebenden Folgen
   - Zur Sprache:
   - stichpunktartige Notizform
   - Verwendung des Präsens soweit möglich
   - Zur Darstellungsform:
   - strukturierte Übersicht erscheint am besten geeignet
   - Erhöhung der Aussagekraft durch z. B. Symbol der Krone, Pfeile etc.

2. – Zum Inhalt: Nennung der Argumente, mit denen der Thronanspruch gerechtfertigt wird, geordnet nach den Thronanwärtern
   - Zur Sprache: stichpunktartige Aufzählung der Argumente
   - Zur Darstellungsform:
   - strukturierte Übersicht und tabellarische Form erscheinen am besten geeignet
   - räumliche Abgrenzung der Thronanwärter

B Creative writing

- Zum Inhalt:
  - Vervollständigen des Antwortbriefes
  - Zurückweisung der Aufforderung zum Rücktritt
  - Rechtfertigung des eigenen Thronanspruches
- Zur Sprache:
  - förmlich und höflich
  - Verwendung von Sprichwörtern, sprachlichen Bildern und christlichem Wortschatz
  - angemessenes Anreden (z. B. "Your Royal Highness/Your Majesty")

Vocabulary

accession	Übernahme, Antritt	*(to) proclaim*	öffentlich erklären
advice	Ratschlag	*(to) promise*	versprechen
approval	Billigung, Genehmigung	*(to) recognize*	anerkennen
(to) await	erwarten	*(to) recommend*	(sich) empfehlen
brave	mutig	*(to) reconsider*	überdenken
brief	kurz	*(to) refuse*	sich weigern
brother-in-law	Schwager	*reign*	Herrschaft
bulletin	offizielle Mitteilung	*(to) remind*	jdn. an etwas erinnern
(to) cause/ cause	verurachen/Ursache	*(to) reply/reply*	anworten/Antwort
(to) claim/ claim	beanspruchen/ Anspruch	*resignation*	Rücktritt, Abdankung
(to) hand down	vererben	*righteousness*	Rechtschaffenheit
heir	Erbe	*rightful*	rechtmäßig
honesty (is the best policy)	Ehrlichkeit (währt am längsten)	*safe and sound*	gesund und munter
honourable	ehrenwert	*salute*	Gruß
justice	Gerechtigkeit	*successor*	Nachfolger
late	hier: verstorbener	*(to) swear*	schwören
pride (goes before a fall)	Hochmut (kommt vor den Fall)	*Thane*	Gefolgsadliger
		well-organized	logisch geordnet
		Witan	Gruppe von einflussreichen Männern, die über den Thronfolger mitentscheiden konnten

Lösungen

A Working on the text

1. ***Hinweise:*** *Die Aufgabe beinhaltet eine kurze und logisch strukturierte Darstellung des Konflikts, der durch König Edwards Tod ausgelöst wird. Der Text beleuchtet diesen Konflikt von drei Seiten: zum einen wird der Konflikt erläutert, zum anderen wird auf Ursachen verwiesen und schließlich werden die Folgen genannt, die sich daraus ergeben. Für die Lösung der Aufgabe bedeutet das, auch alle drei Seiten in der Antwort zu berücksichtigen. Lesen Sie den Text daher gezielt unter diesen Aspekten und markieren Sie systematisch alle relevanten Informationen. Dann ordnen Sie die markierten Informationen den einzelnen Aspekten zu: vermerken Sie an den entsprechenden Textstellen z. B. „K" für den Konflikt, „U" für seine Ursachen und „F" für die Folgen. Nun formulieren Sie den Konflikt (unklare Thronfolge) und stellen die Zusammenhänge her zwischen Ursachen und Folgen.*

Schlüsseltextstellen:

– *Konflikt:*
"Edward the Confessor, King of England, is 61 years old, <u>childless</u> and very sick. When he dies on January 5, there is <u>no direct heir</u> to the English throne. Moreover, Edward has <u>not proclaimed any successor</u> to the throne, <u>which causes trouble</u> as three men claim the English crown ..." (ll. 1–9)

– *Ursachen:*
"Edward the Confessor, King of England, is 61 years old, <u>childless</u> and very sick. When he dies on January 5, there is <u>no direct heir to the English throne</u>. Moreover, Edward has <u>not proclaimed any successor to the throne</u>, which causes trouble as three men claim the English crown ..." (ll. 1–9)

– *Folgen:*
"... which causes trouble as <u>three men claim the English crown: Harold Godwinson, Harold Hardrada and William of Normandy all consider themselves to be the rightful successor.</u>" (ll. 9–12)

Darstellungsform:

Die strukturierte Übersicht ist die am besten geeignete Darstellungsform für diese Aufgabe, da so die Zusammenhänge zwischen Konflikt, Ursachen und Folgen verdeutlicht werden können. Die nachfolgende Lösung ist eine von mehreren Möglichkeiten. Generell wichtig ist, dass die gewählte Form die inhaltliche Aussage bestmöglich unterstützt. Farbliche Hervorhebungen, Symbole und Pfeile können weiterhin eingesetzt werden für eine Erhöhung der Aussagekraft bzw. das Verdeutlichen von Zusammenhängen. In jedem Fall muss das Thema der Aufgabe den Aufzeichnungen vorangestellt werden.

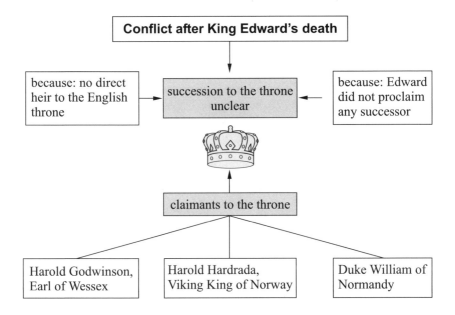

2. **Hinweise:** Die Aufgabe besteht in einer knappen Nennung der Argumente, mit denen die Thronansprüche der Thronanwärter gerechtfertigt werden. Lesen Sie die entsprechenden Textabschnitte gezielt, markieren Sie alle Argumente und ordnen Sie diese nach den drei Thronanwärtern.

Schlüsseltextstellen:

– Harold Godwinson:
"Harold Godwinson, Earl of Wessex, is the <u>most powerful man in England</u>, for Wessex is the richest and most important area at this time. He is <u>a brave and respected leader</u> and <u>the favourite of many English Thanes</u>. He is <u>Edward's brother-in-law</u> and <u>swears that Edward promised him the crown</u> on his deathbed." (ll. 13–16)

– Harold Hardrada:
"Harold Hardrada (also known as Harold III), the <u>powerful Viking King of Norway</u>, <u>claims that his father and his descendants had been promised the English throne</u> by King Hardicanute in 1042." (ll. 17–19)

– Duke William of Normandy:
"Duke William of Normandy, whose <u>family often supported Edward in the past</u>, is a son of Edward's first cousin and therefore the <u>closest blood relation to the late king</u>." (ll. 20–22)

Darstellungsform:

Strukturierte Übersicht und tabellarische Form bieten sich bei dieser Aufgabe an, da lediglich Argumente aufzuzählen sind, geordnet nach den drei Personen. Wichtig ist, diese räumlich voneinander abzugrenzen und/oder gegenüberzustellen, da es sich um Gegenspieler handelt. Außerdem müssen die Aufzeichnungen eine Themanennung/Überschrift (z. B. "Arguments in favour of the succession to the English throne" oder "Reasons why the claimants consider themselves to be the rightful successors to the English throne") erhalten. Nachfolgende Lösung ist wiederum als Vorschlag zu betrachten.

Arguments in favour of the succession to the English throne

Harold Godwinson	Harold Hardrada	Duke William of Normandy
– most powerful man in England – a brave and respected leader – favourite of many Thanes – Edward's brother-in-law – swears that he was promised the throne by Edward	– powerful Viking King of Norway – claims that his father and his descendants had been promised the English throne	– closest blood relation to the late king – family often helped Edward in the past

B Creative writing

Hinweise: Aufgabe ist es, einen Antwortbrief an den Wikingerkönig zu verfassen. Bevor Sie mit dem Entwurf beginnen, lesen Sie den Brief Harold Hardradas genau. Versetzen Sie sich in die Situation von Harold II und versuchen Sie, seine Empörung über die unerhörten Zeilen des Wikingerkönigs nachzuvollziehen. Selbstverständlich geht es im Antwortschreiben zunächst um die Zurückweisung der Rücktrittsforderung. Ferner ist eine Rechtfertigung des eigenen Thronanspruches notwendig. Nutzen Sie dazu verschiedenste Textaussagen und ihre Notizen aus Aufgabe 2. Aufgrund der Standesebene beider Personen ist der zu verfassende Brief sehr höflich und förmlich abzufassen. Missfallensäußerungen werden nur sehr abgeschwächt formuliert und Drohungen verschleiert. Typisch für Briefe in jener Zeit war die Verwendung von sprachlichen Bildern und Sprichwörtern. Für Harolds Antwortbrief eignet sich auch christlicher Wortschatz. Die Wikinger hingegen befanden sich zu diesem Zeitpunkt noch im Christianisierungsprozess, und der Einfluss des Christentums war noch nicht so deutlich spürbar.

… and We kindly ask Your Royal Highness to reconsider Your advice.

We would like to remind Your Majesty of the promise to the crown Our late King Edward and dear brother-in-law made to Us on his deathbed. We would also like to ask Your Highness to respect the decision of the Honourable Witan who approved of Us, Harold II, as the rightful successor to the English throne. Moreover, Our Honourable Thanes have implicit trust in Our reign and support Us without reservation.

Your Majesty will understand that We do not have reason to follow Your call to hand over the crown to You. If Your Highness do not wish to accept Our rightful accession, let fate take its course and may the Lord be with the righteous.

Rest assured of due reception if Your Majesty choose to pay Your royal respects to Us.

With kind salutes

Harold II

Written the Nineteenth day of February in the Year of Our Lord One Thousand and Sixty-Six and in the first Year of Our Reign.

> **Besondere Leistungsfeststellung Thüringen 10. Klasse Englisch**
> **Übungsaufgabe 2**

In the summer of 1066

Harold Hardrada and his men arrive in 300 ships on the Northumbrian coast and invade the north of England. King Harold Godwinson has to stop the Vikings if he wants to remain king and soon marches north. Early in the morning of 25 September 1066
5 the king's troops surprise the Vikings who have not expected an attack so soon. At the end of the day Hardrada's troops are cut to pieces. The Vikings are defeated and Harold Hardrada is killed in the Battle of Stamford Bridge.

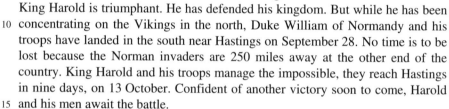

King Harold is triumphant. He has defended his kingdom. But while he has been
10 concentrating on the Vikings in the north, Duke William of Normandy and his troops have landed in the south near Hastings on September 28. No time is to be lost because the Norman invaders are 250 miles away at the other end of the country. King Harold and his troops manage the impossible, they reach Hastings in nine days, on 13 October. Confident of another victory soon to come, Harold
15 and his men await the battle.
However, at the end of the following day England will never be the same again.
At 9.30 the battle begins.
The troops on both sides are about the same size. The battle line of the Normans is at the bottom of a hill. They are at a disadvantage because they have to fight
20 uphill. On the other hand, Harold's troops, who fight downhill, are exhausted from

10

the long march. Until around midday there is fierce fighting on both sides. Then
a rumour goes round that the Duke of Normandy is dead. When in the early afternoon the Normans begin to retreat, King Harold's troops try to overrun them. But
within minutes they are surrounded by hundreds of Normans on horses. Now the
25 Normans' attack is successful. Then King Harold is killed and without their leader
his men have little chance. By the evening the battle is over. Many thousands
have died and William has won the crown of England.

In the Battle of Hastings (as it was called later) on 14 October 1066 the Normans
defeat King Harold's troops. William of Normandy is crowned King of England
30 in Westminster Abbey, London on 24 December the same year.

A Working on the text:
Reading comprehension and organizing information   (25 BE)

1. Show in a brief and suitable way the historic events which finally led
   to William of Normandy being crowned King of England, beginning
   with: 6 January 1066 – Harold Godwinson crowned King Harold II.

2. Explain in a few sentences why the outcome of the Battle of Hastings
   seemed uncertain for a while and how a rumour finally ended in King
   Harold's defeat.

3. Summarize the historic events of autumn 1066 in a few sentences.

B Creative writing   (25 BE)

Oyez, Oyez, Oyez!

Me lords, ladies and good citizens within my voice. Let it be
known to all persons gathered here that Harold II, by the Grace
of God, King of England ...

God rest our late King.

Imagine it is the fifteenth day in the month of October, in the year of our Lord,
one thousand and sixty-six and you are a London town crier who reads the news
to the people of London. Make up the news script in which you inform the Londoners of the main events from the twenty-eighth day of September to the fourteenth day of October, in the year of our Lord, one thousand and sixty-six. The
part of the news script above shows you how to begin and end.

11

Tipps zum Lösungsansatz

A Working on the text

1. – Zum Inhalt:
   - Darstellung der entscheidenden Ereignisse nach dem 6. Januar 1066, die letztendlich die Thronbesteigung durch Wilhelm den Eroberer zur Folge haben
   - Beachtung des vorgegebenen Beginns
   - Nennung aller wichtigen Daten mit dazugehörigen Ereignissen
   – Zur Sprache:
   - Nominalisierung (soweit möglich und sinnvoll) bzw. stichpunktartige Notizform
   - Verwendung des Präsens
   – Zur Darstellungsform: chronologische Zeitleiste am besten geeignet

2. – Zum Inhalt:
   - Eingehen auf Truppenstärke und Kampfbedingungen
   - Rückschlüsse ziehen auf mögliche Missdeutung des Kampfgeschehens
   – Zur Sprache:
   - zusammenhängende Textform
   - Verwendung des Präteritums

3. – Zum Inhalt:
   - Beschränkung auf Wesentliches
   - kurze Verweise auf Hauptereignisse des Frühherbstes
   - Nennung des Ergebnisses dieser Ereignisse
   – Zur Sprache:
   - zusammenhängende Textform
   - Verwendung des Präsens

B Creative writing

– Zum Inhalt:
- zunächst Nennung der wichtigsten Botschaft (wichtigstes Ereignisses und wichtigste Folge)
- knappe Erklärung der Ereignisse im Einzelnen und deren Hintergründe, Folgen und Ergebnisse
- Beachtung der Fasslichkeit der Aussagen, z. B. weitestgehend chronologische Reihenfolge, Erklärung notwendiger Zusammenhänge, Begrenzung des Umfangs

– Zur Sprache:
- zusammenhängende Textform
- einfacher Satzbau
- förmlicher Stil
- typische Redewendungen (siehe Skriptauszug und Aufgabenstellung)

Vocabulary

(to) await	erwarten	*(to) include*	einbeziehen, einschließen
battle	Schlacht	*(to) invade*	einfallen, eindringen
bottom	Boden, Fuß (eines Berges)	*(to) march/* *march*	marschieren/Marsch
brief	kurz	*Oyez, Oyez,*	Hört, hört, hört!
citizen	Bürger	*Oyez!*	
confident of	überzeugt von	*outcome*	Ergebnis, Folge
(to) cut to pieces	in Stücke reißen	*(to) remain*	bleiben
(to) defeat	besiegen	*(to) retreat*	sich zurückziehen
(to) defend	verteidigen	*rumour*	Gerücht
disadvantage	Nachteil	*script*	Skript, Textvorlage
event	Ereignis	*to seem*	Anschein erwecken
exhausted	erschöpft	*(to) surprise*	überraschen
(to) expect	erwarten	*(to) surround*	umringen
fierce	wild, wütend	*town crier*	Ausrufer
(to) gather	versammeln	*troop*	Truppe
God rest our late King.	Der Herr habe unseren verstorbenen König selig.	*victory*	Sieg
		voice	hier: Rufweite

Lösungen

A Working on the text

1. **Hinweise:** *Die Aufgabe besteht in der knappen Darstellung der historischen Ereignisse, die letztendlich zur Thronbesteigung durch Wilhelm den Eroberer führten. Der vorgegebene Beginn ("6 January 1066 – Harold Godwinson crowned King Harold II") ist Ausgangspunkt der Notizen und verweist schon auf das typische Notieren geschichtlicher Ereignisse: Datumsangabe gekoppelt mit dazugehörigem geschichtlichen Fakt. Die Fakten sind möglichst knapp und vorrangig im Präsens zu formulieren, ggf. bietet sich die Nominalisierung an (z. B. Tod König Harold Hardradas). Lesen Sie den Text suchend nach alle entscheidenden Daten und Fakten und markieren Sie diese. Falls nötig, ordnen Sie chronologisch.*

Schlüsseltextstellen:

"In the <u>summer of 1066</u> <u>Harold Hardrada and his men</u> arrive in 300 ships on the Northumbrian coast and <u>invade the north of England</u>." (ll. 1/2)

"Early in the morning of <u>25 September 1066</u> the king's troops surprise the Vikings who have not expected an attack so soon. <u>At the end of the day</u> Hardrada's troops are cut to pieces. The <u>Vikings</u> are <u>defeated</u> and <u>Harold Hardrada</u> is <u>killed</u> in the <u>Battle of Stamford Bridge</u>. (ll. 4–8)

"But while he has been concentrating on the Vikings in the north, <u>Duke William of Normandy and his troops</u> have <u>landed in the south near Hastings on September 28</u>." (ll. 9–11)

"<u>King Harold and his troops</u> manage the impossible, they <u>reach Hastings</u> in nine days, <u>on 13 October</u>." (ll. 13–14)

"In the <u>Battle of Hastings</u> (as it was called later) on <u>14 October 1066</u> the <u>Normans defeat King Harold's troops</u>." (ll. 28/29)

"Then <u>King Harold is killed</u> and without their leader his men have little chance." (l. 25/26)

"<u>William of Normandy</u> is <u>crowned King of England</u> in Westminster Abbey, <u>London on 24 December the same year</u>." (ll. 29/30)

Darstellungsform:

Die Zeitleiste/der Zeitstrahl bietet sich als Notizform an, horizontal oder vertikal angelegt je nach Papierformat.

6 January 1066	Harold Godwinson crowned King Harold II
summer of 1066	Harold Hardrada, Viking King of Norway, and his men invade the north of England
25 September 1066	Battle of Stamford Bridge: Harold II defeats the Vikings, death of King Harold Hardrada
28 September 1066	Duke William of Normandy and his troops land near Hastings
13 October 1066	King Harold and his men reach Hastings
14 October 1066	Battle of Hastings: Normans defeat King Harold's troops, death of Harold II
24 December 1066	William of Normandy crowned King of England

2. *Hinweise: Die Lösung der Aufgabe erfordert jetzt das Lesen „zwischen den Zeilen", d. h. interpretierendes Lesen, da Sie Sachverhalte erklären und deuten sollen. Lesen Sie den Textabschnitt genau und markieren Sie alle relevanten Informationen zum ungewissen Kampfverlauf, d. h. zur Truppenstärke und zu den Kampfbedingungen sowie zum Gerücht und seinen Folgen. Vergleichen Sie die Truppenstärken und stellen Sie die Kampfbedingungen in Ihrer Antwort gegenüber. Deuten Sie mögliche Wirkungen, die das Gerücht um Williams Tod auf die gegnerische Partei gehabt haben könnte. Vermuten Sie, welche Absicht eventuell hinter diesem Gerücht gesteckt haben könnte, insbesondere im Zusammenhang mit dem Rückzug der Normannen. Verfassen Sie Ihre Antwort in einem zusammenhängenden Text und verwenden Sie das Präteritum, da Sie jetzt über etwas Vergangenes reflektieren.*

Schlüsseltextstellen:

"The troops on both sides are about the same size." (ll. 17)

"The battle line of the <u>Normans</u> is at the bottom of a hill. They are at a <u>disadvantage</u> because they <u>have to fight uphill</u>. On the other hand, <u>Harold's troops</u>, who fight downhill, are <u>exhausted from the long march</u>." (ll. 17–21)

"<u>Then a rumour goes round that the Duke of Normandy is dead. When in the early afternoon the Normans begin to retreat, King Harold's troops try to overrun them. But within minutes they are surrounded by hundreds of Normans on horses. Now the Normans' attack is successful</u>." (ll. 21–25)

The outcome of the Battle of Hastings seemed uncertain for a while because the troops on both sides were about the same size. Furthermore, both troops were handicapped: while the Normans had to fight uphill, King Harold's troops were exhausted from the long march. The rumour of William's death, maybe a trap, probably decided the battle because King Harold possibly took both the rumour and the Normans' retreat at face value and underrated the strength of the opponent. Instead of overrunning the retreating enemy, Harold's troops walked right into an unexpected counterattack and were defeated.

3. *Hinweise: Gegenstand der Aufgabe ist eine Zusammenfassung der Ereignisse des Herbstes 1066. Eine Zusammenfassung erstellen ist wie eine Gratwanderung, bei der der Pfad zwischen noch notwendiger und schon überflüssiger Information sehr schmal ist. Deswegen stellen Sie sich beim Notieren für jeden neuen Fakt die Frage, ob die Information zwingend notwendig ist für das Verständnis des Gesamtzusammenhangs. Erwähnensbedürftig sind die Wikinger-Invasion und deren Ergebnis sowie die Invasion der Normannen und deren Ergebnis und Folge. Knappheit und Kürze der Aussage wird weiterhin durch sprachliche Verdichtung erreicht (z. B. "On 25 September, 1066 Harold II repulses the Viking invasion of the north of England ...", "The Norman invasion of the south on 28 September forces Harold ..."). Wie bei einer historischen Zeitleiste wird auch bei einer Zusammenfassung geschichtlicher Ereignisse Vergangenes in die Gegenwart geholt und das Präsens verwendet.*

On 25 September, 1066 Harold II repulses the Viking invasion of the north of England in the Battle of Stamford Bridge. The Norman invasion of the south on 28 September forces Harold and his troops to rush to the next battlefield. Yet, King Harold II is out of luck and is defeated by William in the Battle of Hastings on 14 October. William of Normandy is crowned King of England on 24 December the same year.

B Creative writing

Hinweise: Aufgabe ist, den Nachrichtentext des Ausrufers zu erstellen, und zwar für den Zeitraum vom 28. 09. bis 14. 10. 1066.

Bekanntmachungen in jener Zeit waren für die überwiegende Mehrheit der Bevölkerung, die weder schreiben noch lesen konnte, die einzige offizielle Nachrichtenquelle und somit von entscheidender Bedeutsamkeit. Ausrufer waren in der Regel vornehme und gebildete Personen von Rang und Stand, die dieses „Handwerk" regelrecht erlernten. Zu ihren Aufgaben gehörte es, die Nachrichtentexte sprachlich so zu gestalten, dass sie von der Zuhörerschaft gut erfasst und richtig weitergegeben werden konnten. Entsprechend galt es, bestimmte Regeln zu beachten: klarer, leicht fasslicher Inhalt, begrenzter Umfang, förmlicher Stil und sprachlich einfacher Satzbau. Dieses sollten Sie so weit wie möglich berücksichtigen. Nutzen Sie für Ihre Lösung den in dem Skriptauszug vorgegebenen Anfangs- und Endtext, der typisch für Bekanntmachungen in jener Zeit ist. Beachten Sie auch die Art der Zeitangabe in der Aufgabenstellung.

Bei der Erstellung des Nachrichtentextes versuchen Sie nun, sich in die Situation der englischen Bevölkerung zu versetzen, deren Heimatland von fremden Eindringlingen bedroht wurde und die nach dem Sieg über Harold Hardrada auch auf erfolgreiche Abwehr des Feindes im Süden hofften.

Nennen Sie zunächst klar und deutlich die wichtigste Botschaft für die damalige Bevölkerung: der Tod Harold II und die Machtübernahme durch den Eindringling, Wilhelm den Eroberer. Dann sollten knapp Ereignisse erläutert werden, die zwischen dem Sieg über die Wikinger und der nächsten Schlacht lagen, insbesondere jene, die wahrscheinlich Einfluss auf den Ausgang der Schlacht bei Hastings hatten (Erschöpfung von der Schlacht bei Stamford Bridge, Eilmarsch nach Hastings). Der Kampfverlauf der Schlacht bei Hastings sollte etwas detaillierter erläutert werden, da dies für die Zuhörerschaft in jener Zeit besonders interessant gewesen sein dürfte. Versuchen Sie auch, auf deren Gefühle etwas Rücksicht zu nehmen. Abschließend nennen Sie noch einmal das entscheidende Ergebnis: die Machtübernahme durch den Normannen Wilhelm.

Oyez, Oyez, Oyez!
Me lords, ladies and good citizens within my voice. Let it be known to all persons gathered here that Harold II, by the Grace of God, King of England, is dead. He died heroically in the battle against the Normans on the fourteenth day of October, this year of our Lord one thousand and sixty-six. God rest his soul. Our homeland has fallen under Norman sway.

Let it be recalled that after their glorious victory over the Vikings, King Harold and his forces could not allow themselves well-deserved rest. Instead, our brave warriors had to rush south because Duke William of Normandy and his troops had landed near Hastings. Harold and his men covered the 250 miles to Hastings in only nine days, and arrived there on the thirteenth day of October.

On the morning of the fourteenth day of October, the battle began. Until around midday there was fierce fighting on both sides and the outcome of the battle seemed uncertain for a while. Yet, in the afternoon the tide turned and Fortune let Harold down. While trying to overrun the Normans, our warriors were ambushed and King Harold, God rest his soul, was killed. Despite supreme effort, once King Harold was dead, our men were fighting a losing battle.

By the evening, the battle was lost, with thousands of our brave brothers dead. May their souls rest in peace.

William of Normandy has taken over control of our homeland and may be expected here in London at any time.

God rest our late King."

> **Besondere Leistungsfeststellung Thüringen 10. Klasse Englisch**
> **Übungsaufgabe 3**

Teenage moods

What is natural and what is not?

Teenage mood swings, poor performance at school and strange behaviour can all be a normal part of growing up – but sometimes they are symptoms of serious emotional or mental problems needing professional help. How can you find out the difference? What is normal behaviour and what is a sign that something is wrong?

16-year-old Molly believes 'everyone' hates her. She says the classmates she hangs around with at school are mean to her, her teachers treat her unfairly and her parents criticise her all the time.

17-year-old Vanessa assumes people are plotting to harm her – she is often scared that she is being followed or that people are trying to poison her food.

David's parents are concerned about their teenage son, who has been "down" for the last few days. When they want to know what is wrong, he snaps, 'Leave me alone!' and walks off to his room.

Robert's parents are worried too. Their 16-year-old son spends all afternoon and evening in his room alone and has been doing so for several weeks. His parents feel he is withdrawing into his shell more and more – he is not only isolating himself from his family, but has stopped seeing his friends, too. He is doing poorly at school, even though he used to be quite a good student.

Molly's idea that nobody seems to like her sounds like a typical teenage feeling, but Vanessa's fears may be of a more serious nature – she may be suffering from a persecution complex. If David is back to his usual cheerful self in a few days, he is probably having normal teenage mood swings. But Robert needs help – he seems to be seriously depressed.

When is professional help needed?

Here are some types of behaviour that call for professional treatment if they occur regularly or constantly over a long period of time:

A persecution complex – such as the fear of being followed, or the idea that someone wants to harm you – is a symptom that should be taken seriously. Another sign that shows that something is wrong is unusual thoughts, e. g. when someone has the feeling that the radio or TV is controlling them, or supposes they can read other people's minds and that other people can read their minds. Moreover, confused thinking, constant feelings of sadness and fear, lack of concentration, and a very noticeable change in sleep pattern indicate that treatment is necessary.

Sometimes these symptoms may be caused by a specific illness, but they may also be an aftereffect of a severe crisis in the young person's life. Bereavement, a serious illness or injury or sexual abuse, for instance, may bring about a traumatic shock. Moreover, some symptoms can be a reaction to taking an illegal drug. The important thing is to contact a health professional immediately.

A Working on the text:
Reading comprehension and organizing information   (25 BE)

1. Compare in a short and well-structured way the behavioural problems the four different teenagers have and mention briefly how these problems should be seen.

2. Demonstrate briefly and in a well-organized manner when behavioural problems make professional help necessary. Include the following aspects: preconditions, behavioural symptoms and possible causes.

B Creative writing   (25 BE)

How moody are you?
Draw up a questionnaire for teenagers on the topic *How moody are you?* Include a suitable answer pattern, a system of points and an interpretation of the results.

Tipps zum Lösungsansatz

A Working on the text

1. – Zum Inhalt:
   - Nennung der einzelnen Verhaltensauffälligkeiten geordnet nach den Personen
   - Darstellung, wie diese zu bewerten sind
   – Zur Sprache: stichpunktartige Notizform
   – Zur Darstellungsform: Tabelle am besten geeignet

2. – Zum Inhalt:
   - Darstellung der Verhaltensauffälligkeiten, die professionelle Hilfe erfordern
   - Nennung der einzelnen Voraussetzungen, Verhaltenssymptome und möglichen Ursachen
   – Zur Sprache: stichpunktartige Notizform
   – Zur Darstellungsform: Mind Map am besten geeignet

B Creative writing

– Zum Inhalt:
   - zahlreiche Entscheidungsfragen, die launisches Verhalten erfragen
   - Antwortschema: z. B. geordnet nach Häufigkeit von immer bis nie
   - Punktesystem: z. B. Bepunktung in Abhängigkeit von der Häufigkeit
   - Ergebniserläuterung: Klassifizierung in Schritten mit entsprechender Punktezuordnung von z. B. „Glückwunsch!" bis „Höchste Zeit, etwas zu ändern!" und Kommentierung
– Zur Sprache: stilistisch ungefärbt bis jugendlich salopp

Vocabulary

abuse	Missbrauch	*pattern*	Muster, Gewohnheit
(to) assume	annehmen	*(to) occur*	auftreten
behaviour/	Verhalten/Verhaltens-	*particular*	spezielle
behavioural		*performance*	Leistung
bereavement	schmerzlicher Verlust	*persecution*	Verfolgung
cheerful self	heiteres Ich	*(to) prefer*	bevorzugen
complex	Komplex, Wahn	*(to) plot*	sich verschwören
(to be) concerned	besorgt sein	*professional*	Experte
confused	verwirrt	*sad/sadness*	traurig/Traurigkeit
depressed	depressiv	*(to be) scared*	Angst haben
(to) grow up	aufwachsen	*serious/(to) take*	ernsthaft/etwas ernst
(to) harm so.	jdm. schaden	*sth. seriously*	nehmen
immediately	sofort	*shell*	Schale, Hülle
lack	Mangel	*sleep pattern*	Schlafgewohnheiten
(to) leave so.	jdn. in Ruhe lassen	*(to) snap*	anschnauzen
alone		*strange*	seltsam
loss	Verlust	*(to) suffer from*	leiden unter
mean	gemein	*traumatic*	traumatisch, seelisch
mind	hier: Gedanke	*(to) treat/*	behandeln/
mood	Stimmung	*treatment*	Behandlung
mood swing	Stimmungsschwankung	*(to) withdraw*	zurückziehen
noticeable	auffällig	*(to be ~) worried*	besorgt (sein)

Lösungen

A Working on the text

1. *Hinweise: Die Aufgabe besteht in der Nennung der Verhaltensauffälligkeiten der vier Jugendlichen. Lesen Sie die Aussagen zu den einzelnen Jugendlichen detailliert und markieren Sie alle entsprechenden Textstellen zu deren Verhalten. Kennzeichnen Sie auch, wie die einzelnen Auffälligkeiten bewertet werden. Beim Notieren bemühen Sie sich um stichpunktartige Notizform.*

Schlüsseltextstellen:

– *Molly:*

"16-year-old Molly <u>believes 'everyone' hates her</u>. She <u>says the classmates</u> she hangs around with at school are <u>mean to her</u>, her <u>teachers treat her unfairly</u> and <u>her parents criticise her</u> all the time." (ll. 10–12)
"Molly's idea that nobody seems to like her sounds like <u>a typical teenage feeling</u>, …" (ll. 25/26)

- *Vanessa:*
  "17-year-old Vanessa <u>assumes people are plotting to harm her</u> – she is <u>often scared that she is being followed</u> or that <u>people are trying to poison her food.</u>" (ll. 13/14)
  "... but Vanessa's fears may be <u>of a more serious nature</u> – she <u>may be suffering from a persecution complex.</u>" (ll. 26–28)

- *David:*
  "David's parents are concerned about their teenage son, who <u>has been 'down' for the last few days</u>. When they want to know what is wrong, he snaps, 'Leave me alone!' and walks off to his room." (ll. 15–17)
  "If David is back to his usual cheerful self in a few days, he is <u>probably having normal teenage mood swings.</u>" (ll. 28/29)

- *Robert:*
  "Robert's parents are worried too. Their 16-year-old son <u>spends all afternoon and evening in his room alone</u> and <u>has been doing so for several weeks</u>. His parents feel he is <u>withdrawing into his shell more and more</u> – he is <u>not only isolating himself from his family</u>, but has <u>stopped seeing his friends</u>, too. He is <u>doing poorly at school</u>, even though he <u>used to be quite a good student.</u>" (ll. 18–24)
  "But Robert needs help – he seems to be seriously depressed." (l. 29/30)

Darstellungsform:
Vergleiche lassen sich in der Regel sehr effektiv in tabellarischer Form ausführen. Wählen Sie geeignete Spalten- und Zeilenbezeichnungen. Bei dem Vermerken, wie die Probleme zu betrachten sind, ist ein weiteres Untergliedern in normale und ernsthafte emotionale Probleme möglich.

	Behavioural problems	Problems should be seen as	
		normal emotional problems	serious emotional problems
Molly	– thinks everyone hates her – says classmates are mean to her, teachers treat her unfairly, parents criticise her all the time	a typical teenage feeling	—
Vanessa	– thinks people are plotting to harm her – scared that people are following her or trying to poison her food	—	may be suffering from a persecution complex
David	– has been "down" for the last few days	probably having normal teenage mood swings	—
Robert	– spends hours in his room alone – has been doing so for many weeks – withdrawing more and more into his shell – not only withdrawing from his family – stopped seeing his friends, too – doing badly at school – used to be a good student	—	seems to be seriously depressed

2. *Hinweise: Ziel der Aufgabe ist das knappe und logisch geordnete Darstellen der Zusammenhänge, wann Verhaltensauffälligkeiten der fachmännischen Hilfe bedürfen. Dabei sind drei Hauptpunkte zu beachten: Voraussetzungen, Symptome und mögliche Ursachen. Lesen Sie die entsprechenden Textabschnitte genau und markieren Sie alle relevanten Informationen. Ordnen Sie diese parallel durch kurze Vermerke wie z. B. „V", „S" und „U" gleich den genannten Hauptpunkten zu.*

Schlüsseltextstellen:

– *preconditions:*
   "Here are some types of behaviour that call for professional treatment if they occur regularly or constantly over a long period of time" (ll. 32/33)
– *symptoms:*
   "A persecution complex – such as the fear of being followed, or the idea that someone wants to harm you – is a symptom that should be taken seriously." (ll. 34–36)

"Another sign that shows that something is wrong is <u>unusual thoughts</u>, e. g. when someone has the <u>feeling that the radio or TV is controlling them</u>, or <u>supposes they can read other people's minds and that other people can read their minds</u>." (ll. 36–40)
"Moreover, <u>confused thinking</u>, <u>constant feelings of sadness and fear</u>, <u>lack of concentration</u>, and a <u>very noticeable change in sleep pattern</u> indicate that treatment is necessary." (ll. 40–42)

– *possible causes:*
"Sometimes these symptoms may be caused by a <u>specific illness</u>, but they may also be an <u>aftereffect of a severe crisis</u> in the young person's life. <u>Bereavement</u>, <u>a serious illness or injury</u> or <u>sexual abuse</u>, for instance, may bring about a <u>traumatic shock</u>. Moreover, some symptoms can be a reaction to <u>taking an illegal drug</u>." (ll. 43–50)

Darstellungsform:
Die sehr große Faktenzahl und das notwendige Darstellen von Zusammenhängen erfordern Formen, die diesen Bedingungen gerecht werden können. Solche sind vor allem das Mind Map, die strukturierte Übersicht oder die klassisch nummeriert gegliederte Übersicht. Unabhängig davon, für welche Form Sie sich entscheiden, ist es wichtig, notwendige Unterordnungen der weiterführenden Informationen vorzunehmen bei den Unterpunkten „persecution complex", „unusual thoughts" sowie „aftereffect/traumatic shock". Betiteln Sie Ihre Notizen entsprechend der Aufgabenstellung bzw. vermerken Sie das Thema des Mind Map zentral (z. B. "Behavioural problems that make professional treatment necessary").

Darstellungsform 1: Strukturierte Übersicht
When behavioural problems make professional help necessary
– Preconditions: symptoms occur
  • regularly or constantly
  • over a long period of time
– Symptoms
  • persecution complex
    ▪ fear of being followed
    ▪ idea that someone wants to harm them
  • unusual thoughts
    ▪ feeling that radio/TV is controlling them
    ▪ supposing they can read other people's minds or people can read their minds
  • confused thinking
  • constant feelings of sadness and fear

- lack of concentration
- very noticeable change in sleep pattern
– Possible causes
  - a specific illness
  - aftereffect of a severe crisis/traumatic shock after e. g.:
    - bereavement
    - serious illness or injury
    - sexual abuse
  - taking an illegal drug

Darstellungsform 2: Mind Map

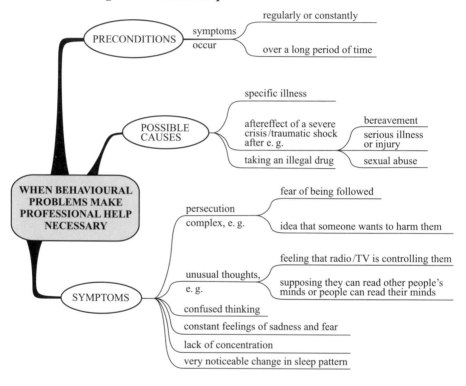

Darstellungsform 3: Nummeriert gegliederte Übersicht

When behavioural problems make professional help necessary

1	**Preconditions:** symptoms occur
1.1	Regularly or constantly
1.2	Over a long period of time
2	**Symptoms**
2.1	Persecution complex, e. g.
2.1.1	Fear of being followed
2.1.2	Idea that someone wants to harm them
2.2	Unusual thoughts, e. g.
2.2.1	Feeling that radio/TV is controlling them
2.2.2	Supposing they can read other people's minds or people can read their minds
2.3	Confused thinking
2.4	Constant feelings of sadness and fear
2.5	Lack of concentration
2.6	Very noticeable change in sleep pattern
3	**Possible causes**
3.1	Specific illness
3.2	Aftereffect of a severe crisis/traumatic shock after e. g. ...
3.2.1	Bereavement
3.2.2	Serious illness or injury
3.2.3	Sexual abuse
3.3	Taking an illegal drug

B Creative writing

Hinweise: Ziel der Aufgabe ist, einen Fragebogen für Jugendliche zu erarbeiten zum Thema „Wie launisch bist du?" Dazu sind parallel ein Antwortschema, ein Punktesystem und eine Ergebniswertung zu erstellen. Tragen Sie zunächst möglichst vielseitige Fragen zum Thema zusammen. Verwenden Sie Entscheidungsfragen mit "Do you ..." oder "Are you ...?" Wenn Sie der Einfachheit halber bei der Fragenformulierung immer von durchgängig positiven oder durchgängig negativen Ansatzpunkten ausgehen, funktioniert die Wertung in Punkteabhängigkeit ohne mühseliges Berechnen. Allerdings ist solches Vorgehen auch leicht durchschaubar! Überlegen Sie, welches Antwortsystem Sie einbinden wollen. Abgestufte Häufigkeitsangaben ("always, almost always, sometimes, seldom, never") bieten sich dabei an. Ordnen Sie den Häufigkeitsangaben entsprechende Punktzahlen zu. Zum Schluss erstellen Sie z. B. in einem Fünferschritt Wertungen und Kommentare und ergänzen die dazugehörige Punktspanne.

How moody are you?

		always	almost always	some times	seldom	never
1.	Do you feel fresh and relaxed when you wake up?	☐	☐	☐	☐	☐
2.	Do you switch on the radio after waking up?	☐	☐	☐	☐	☐
3.	Do you take your time over breakfast?	☐	☐	☐	☐	☐
4.	Do you feel like talking early in the morning?	☐	☐	☐	☐	☐
5.	Can you tolerate noisy or hectic people around you in the morning?	☐	☐	☐	☐	☐
6.	Are you friendly and polite even if someone gets on your nerves?	☐	☐	☐	☐	☐
7.	Do you keep calm when things go wrong?	☐	☐	☐	☐	☐
8.	Do you remain your cheerful self even if someone criticises or opposes you?	☐	☐	☐	☐	☐
9.	Do you accept not being the focus of attention?	☐	☐	☐	☐	☐
10.	Are you composed even if your feelings are hurt?	☐	☐	☐	☐	☐

Scores:

answer	score
always	5 points
almost always	4 points
sometimes	3 points
seldom	2 points
never	no point

What your score means:

40 to 50 points	**Congratulations!**	You are cheerful and easy-going and always seem to be in a good mood.
30 to 39 points	**Not bad!**	Your good mood seldom gets affected by everyday problems.
20 to 29 points	**It's all right!**	On the whole, problems do not influence your mood too much.
10 to 19 points	**Cheer up!**	You sometimes seem to suffer from mood swings. Don't take everything so seriously!
0 to 9 points	**High time for a change!**	Mood swings seem to dominate your personality. You need to understand that everyone has problems of some kind. Try to accept that people have different lifestyles, opinions and ideas.

> **Besondere Leistungsfeststellung Thüringen 10. Klasse Englisch**
> **Übungsaufgabe 4**

Illegal drugs

Illegal drugs like hallucinogens (LSD, marijuana and ecstasy), pain-killers (morphine and heroin), stimulants (speed, cocaine) and common solvents (e. g. glue, paint thinner, petrol) not only cause very serious physical damage to the body, but can affect mental health as well. Besides most of them being dangerously
5 addictive, they can change the mind and personality permanently. Most often psychiatric disorders are depression, suicidal feelings, schizophrenia, personality disorder and alcohol-related problems. Yet, drug abuse is on the increase, especially among young people.
According to DrugScope, about 3 % of 11–12 year olds, 23 % of children aged
10 14–15, and 29 % of young people between 16–24 in England and Wales took an illegal drug in 2001. There has been an increase in the use of cocaine from 6 % of 16–29 year olds who tried the drug in 1998 to 10 % of the same age range who tried it in 2000. Studies in 2000 have revealed that cocaine was preferred to ecstasy. Cannabis (marijuana) was still the most widely consumed illegal drug in
15 the UK in 2000 with 44 % of 16–29 year olds having tried it. This was an increase from 42 % in 1998. Ecstasy use is reported with a small increase from 4 % of 16–29 years olds having tried the drug in 1998 to 5 % in 2000.
One probable reason why the use of marijuana has constantly been on the increase for some years is that people consider it a safe drug. It is not known to
20 be physically addictive, and this seems to make it harmless in the eyes of its users. Moreover, as there are no physical withdrawal symptoms when you stop using it, people are more and more prepared to risk a joint.

Smoking cannabis causes a number of physical effects, such as increased pulse rate, decreased blood pressure, bloodshot eyes or increased appetite, for instance. But it is the drug's effect on your senses and emotions which makes people use it. Pleasant stimulation, feelings of giddiness and euphoria, followed by sedation and pleasant tranquillity are the sensations reported most often.

Whilst under the influence of cannabis, your thinking processes, e. g. your short-term memory or problem-solving ability may be seriously affected. Co-ordination and reaction time can be slowed down, meaning that accidents may be more likely, especially if people drive or operate machinery. Some people find that cannabis makes them very anxious and panicky. This can happen with inexperienced users or if people consume strong varieties or high doses of cannabis. Very heavy use may lead to very distressing experiences such as confusion, panic attacks, feelings of helplessness or loss of self-control.

A **Working on the text:**
  Reading comprehension and organizing information (25 BE)

  1. Illustrate the percentage of young drug takers in England and Wales in 2001 for the different age ranges mentioned in the text and the increase in the use of certain drugs among 16–29 year olds from 1998 to 2000.
  2. Present briefly and in a well-organized way the most important facts about drugs in general (kinds, effects) and cannabis specifically (use, reasons, effects, abuse etc.).

B **Creative writing** (25 BE)

  Choose one of the following tasks. Write a text of at least 200 words.

  1. Inquiring about drugs
     For a presentation you need reliable and authoritative information on drug use and treatment in the UK. Inquire at DrugScope, the UK's leading independent centre of expertise on drugs, about the latest figures in drug use among children and young people, present trends in drug use, drug treatment, organizations providing special drug treatment, care services, self-help groups etc.

postal address:
DrugScope
32–36 Loman St.
London
SE1 0EF

e-mail address:
info@drugscope.org.uk

2. "Don't be a spoilsport! Using marijuana isn't as dangerous as people think; you don't get addicted ..."
   Discuss the influence your peers have on you, and the problem of peer pressure.
   Could you be talked into trying a soft drug like marijuana? Give reasons.

Vocabulary

(to be) addictive	abhängig machend
(to) affect	betreffen, auswirken
anxious	ängstlich, beunruhigt
bloodshot	blutunterlaufen
(to) cause	verursachen
common	gebräuchlich, normal
confusion	Verwirrung
(to) consider	betrachten, halten für
damage	Schaden
decreased	erniedrigt, gesenkt
disorder	Störung
distressing	quälend
effect	(Aus-)Wirkung
euphoria	Hochstimmung
experience	Erfahrung
giddiness	Leichtsinn, Übermut
hallucinogen	Halluzinogen
increase	Steigerung
inexperienced	unerfahren
(to) influence/	beeinflussen/
influence	Einfluss
(to) operate	bedienen
joint	Joint, Marihuana-zigarette
likely	wahrscheinlich

mental	geistig
pain-killer	Schmerzstiller
panicky	überängstlich
peer	Gleichaltriger, Gleichgesinnter
physical	körperlich
(to) prefer	bevorzugen
schizophrenia	Schizophrenie, Bewusstseinsspaltung
sedation	Beruhigung
(to) seem	den Anschein haben
sensation	Empfindung
sense	Sinn
serious	ernsthaft
short-term	Kurzzeit-
solvent	Lösungsmittel
spoilsport	Spielverderber
stimulant/stimulation	Anregungsmittel/Anregung
suicidal	Selbsttötungs-
(to) talk so. into doing sth.	jdn. überreden, etwas zu tun
tranquillity	Ruhe, Gelassenheit
withdrawal symptom	Entzugserscheinung

Lösungen

A Working on the text

1. *Hinweise: Ziel der Aufgabe ist es, Daten zu veranschaulichen. Beachten Sie dabei, dass die Aufgabe aus zwei Teilaufgaben besteht: einmal ist der Prozentsatz an Drogenkonsumenten in England und Wales für das Jahr 2001 in den verschiedenen Altersgruppen bildhaft darzustellen (Teilaufgabe a). Zum anderen sollen Sie den Anstieg in der Einnahme bestimmter Drogen bei den 16- bis 29-Jährigen von 1998 bis 2000 veranschaulichen (Teilaufgabe b). Markieren Sie alle relevanten Prozentangaben und dazugehörigen Fakten im Text. Nutzen Sie unterschiedliche Farben für die Teilaufgaben.*

Schlüsseltextstellen:

– *Teilaufgabe a:*
  "According to DrugScope, <u>about 3 % of 11–12 year olds</u>, <u>23 % of children aged 14–15</u>, and <u>29 % of young people between 16–24</u> in England and Wales took an illegal drug in 2001." (ll. 9–11)

– *Teilaufgabe b:*
  There has been an increase in the use of <u>cocaine from 6 % of 16–29 year olds</u> who tried the drug <u>in 1998</u> to <u>10 % of the same age range</u> who tried it <u>in 2000</u>. Studies in 2000 have revealed that cocaine was preferred to ecstasy. <u>Cannabis (marijuana) was still the most widely consumed illegal drug in the UK in 2000 with 44 % of 16–29 year olds</u> having tried it. This was an increase <u>from 42 % in 1998</u>. <u>Ecstasy</u> use is reported with a small increase <u>from 4 % of 16–29 years</u> olds having tried the drug <u>in 1998</u> to <u>5 % in 2000</u>. (ll. 11–17)

Darstellungsform:

Teilaufgabe a:
Hier erscheinen Kreisdiagramme für die drei unterschiedlichen Altersgruppen sinnvoll, da so das Verhältnis zur jeweiligen Gesamtaltersgruppe (100 %) darstellbar wird. Erstellen Sie also drei Kreisdiagramme mit den jeweiligen Werten und beschriften Sie diese mit den dazugehörigen Altersgruppen und den dargestellten Werten. Nutzen Sie Farben zur Verstärkung der Aussage und finden Sie eine geeignete Überschrift (z. B. "Percentage of young drug takers in England and Wales in 2001").

Teilaufgabe b:
Veränderungen in Daten lassen sich anschaulich in Säulendiagrammen gegenüberstellen. Legen Sie die Werteachse in geeigneten Prozentschritten an und beschriften Sie diese mit „percentage" An der Kategorienachse vermerken Sie die jeweilige der drei im Text erwähnten Drogen. Tragen Sie für jede

33

der drei Drogen die Werte für 1998 und 2000 ein. (Zusätzlich können die Werte an den Säulen vermerkt werden, wenn die Wertaussage aufgrund der Platzverhältnisse nicht eindeutig erscheint.) Weiterhin lässt sich z. B. ein Farbschema für die 1998-Säulen und die 2000-Säulen anwenden, um die Betonung auf die Veränderung zu legen. Nennen Sie in einer Überschrift den Gegenstand Ihrer Darstellung (z. B. "Increase in the use of certain drugs among 16 to 29 year olds in the UK from 1998 to 2000").

Percentage of young drug takers in England and Wales in 2001

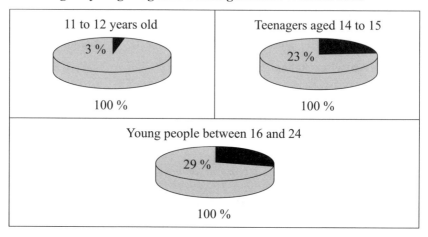

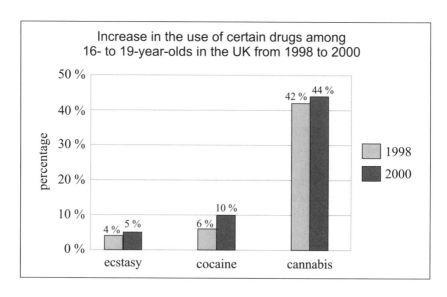

2. **Hinweise:** *Es sind knapp und übersichtlich wesentliche Aussagen über Drogen allgemein und zu Cannabis speziell darzustellen. Beachten Sie die Hinweise in den Klammern, die mögliche Aspekte des Notierens erwähnen. Lesen Sie den Abschnitt zu Drogen allgemein genau und markieren Sie alle notierenswerten Angaben zu Arten und Auswirkungen. Prüfen Sie, welche Unterordnungen sich zu den beiden Aspekten ergeben. Bei Arten kann differenziert werden zwischen illegalen Drogen und handelsüblichen Lösungsmitteln. Die Auswirkungen sind unterteilbar in solche auf den Körper und jene auf den Geist und die Persönlichkeit. Später prüfen Sie, ob diese Unterordnungen ihrerseits ein weiteres Aufgliedern erfordern. Analog gehen Sie bei den Abschnitten zu Cannabis vor. Hier markieren Sie alle wichtigen Fakten zu Einnahme und Auswirkungen. Da die Informationen zu Auswirkungen von Cannabis sehr umfangreich sind, ist sinnvolles Unterordnen geboten. Unterscheiden Sie auch hier zunächst zwischen Auswirkungen auf den Körper und auf die Sinne/Gefühlslage. Weitere erwähnte Auswirkungen sind solche auf den Denkprozess, jene bei unerfahrenen Einnehmern bzw. Stoffstärke/Dosishöhe und jene bei sehr starker Anwendung. Ggf. ist auch bei diesen Unterpunkten ein weiteres Untergliedern erforderlich.*

Schlüsseltexstellen:

Drogen allgemein:

– *Arten*

   "*Illegal drugs like hallucinogens (LSD, marijuana and ecstasy), pain-killers (morphine and heroin), stimulants (speed, cocaine) and common solvents (e. g. glue, paint thinner, petrol) not only cause ...*" *(ll. 1–3)*

– *Auswirkungen*

   • *Auf den Körper:*

   "*... not only cause very serious physical damage to the body, but can affect mental health as well. Besides most of them being dangerously addictive, they can change the mind and personality permanently.*"
   (ll. 3–5)

   • *Auf den Geist und die Persönlichkeit:*

   "*but ... can affect mental health as well. Besides most of them being dangerously addictive, they can change the mind and personality permanently. Most often psychiatric disorders are depression, suicidal feelings, schizophrenia, personality disorder and alcohol-related problems.*"
   (ll. 4–8)

Cannabis speziell:

− *Einnahme:*

"One probable reason why the <u>use</u> of marijuana <u>has constantly been on the increase</u> for some years probably is that <u>people consider it a safe drug</u>. It is <u>not known to be physically addictive</u>, and this seems to make it harmless in the eyes of its users. Moreover, as there are <u>no physical withdrawal symptoms</u> when you stop using it, people are more and more prepared to risk a joint." (ll. 18−22)

− *Auswirkungen*

• *Auf den Körper:*

"Smoking cannabis causes a number of physical effects, such as <u>increased pulse rate, decreased blood pressure, bloodshot eyes</u> or <u>increased appetite</u>, for instance." (ll. 23−27)

• *Auf die Sinne/Gefühlslage:*

"But it is the drug's effect on your senses and emotions which makes people use it. <u>Pleasant stimulation, feelings of giddiness and euphoria, followed by sedation and pleasant tranquillity</u> are the sensations reported most often." (ll. 27−33)

• *Auf den Denkprozess:*

„Whilst under the influence of cannabis, your thinking processes, e. g. your <u>short-term memory</u> or <u>problem-solving ability may be seriously affected. Co-ordination</u> and <u>reaction time can be slowed down</u>, meaning that accidents may be more likely, especially if people drive or operate machinery." (ll. 34−37)

• *Bei unerfahrenen Einnehmern bzw. hoher Stoffstärke und Dosis:*

„Some people find that cannabis makes them very <u>anxious</u> and <u>panicky</u>. This can happen <u>with inexperienced users</u> or if people consume <u>strong varieties or high doses of cannabis</u>." (ll. 37−39)

• *Bei starker Anwendung:*

Very <u>heavy use</u> may lead to very distressing experiences such as <u>confusion, acute panic attacks, feelings of helplessness or loss of self-control</u>. (ll. 39−41)

Darstellungsform:

Aufgrund der enormen Faktenfülle und verschiedener Unterordnungsebenen erscheinen das Mind Map und gegliederte Übersichten am besten geignet. Darüber hinaus ist ein Trennen der beiden Hauptpunkte (Drogen allgemein, Cannabis speziell) für mehr Übersichtlichkeit erwägenswert. Bei ausreichenden Platzverhältnissen, wie z. B. beim Erstellen des Mind Map von Hand, können die gesamten Notizen des Mind Map „Cannabis" im Mind Map „Drugs In General" an entsprechender Stelle angefügt werden.

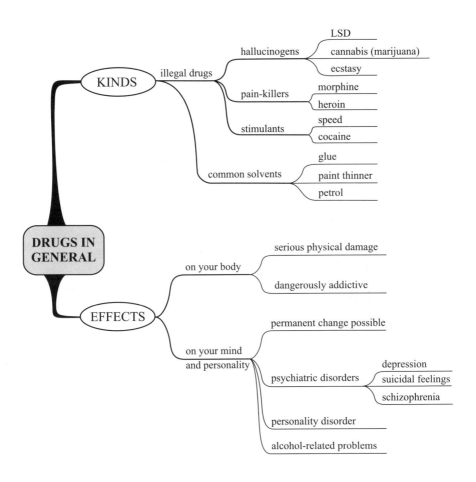

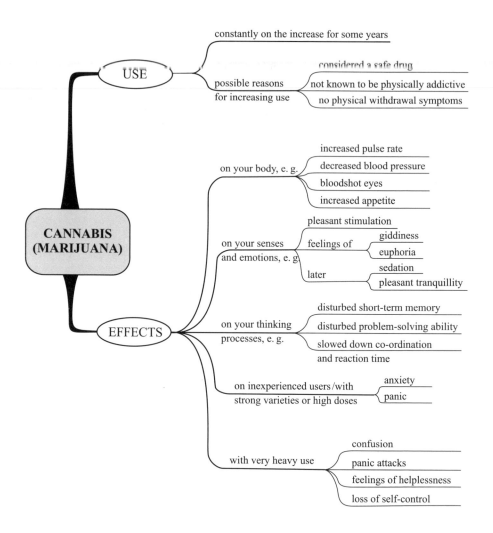

B Creative writing

1. *Hinweise: Die Aufgabe zielt auf das Einholen von Informationen zum Thema Drogen bei der britischen Organisation „DrugScope" ab. In der Aufgabenstellung wird nicht explizit darauf verwiesen, dass ein „formal letter", ein Geschäftsbrief zu erarbeiten ist. Ein Erkundigungsschreiben dieser Art ist aber als solcher abzufassen. Beachten Sie daher die äußeren Merkmale dieser speziellen Briefform. Der Geschäftsbrief ist zunächst in geeigneter Weise einzuleiten, wozu der in der Aufgabenstellung genannte Schreibanlass (die Präsentation) aufgegriffen werden kann. Anschließend formulieren Sie, geordnet nach Abschnitten, die einzelnen Punkte, zu denen Sie Informationen wünschen. Die Aufgabenstellung bietet Ihnen diesbezüglich verschiedene Anregungen. Greifen Sie diese je nach Bedarf auf. Dabei ist mitunter eine Konkretisierung einzelner Punkte notwendig, um dem Brief Sinn zu geben. Weiterhin sollten Sie sich um einen abwechslungsreichen Ausdruck bemühen und möglichst vielfältige Redewendungen zum Einholen von Informationen anwenden. Im Schlusssatz bietet sich ein Bedanken und ein Verweisen auf die Rückantwort an, da die Beantwortung Ihrer Anfragen mit Mühen verbunden sein dürfte.*

Goethestr. 6
07743 Jena
Germany

DrugScope
32–36 Loman St.
London, SE1 0EF
Great Britain

28 October 2003

Dear Sir/Madam

I am writing to you because I am interested in information on drug use and treatment in the UK. I would like to use the information for a school presentation on drug use in the UK and Germany which I will be giving next January.

First, I would like to ask you for the latest figures on the use of different drugs among children and young people in the UK. In a text I read recently I found statistics of yours about the use of several drugs among British teenagers and young people in 2001 and I was wondering if you could supply me with more recent figures.

Second, I would like to inquire about present trends in drug use. Have there been any significant changes in the use of particular drugs, similar to the considerable increase in the use of cocaine you found for the period from 1998 to 2000, for instance.

Furthermore, would it be possible for you to send me information on drug treatment and care services? In this respect I would also be grateful for a list of British organizations which provide special drug treatment.

Finally, I would be very grateful if you could provide me with the names and addresses of some self-help groups. Could you also recommend a self-help group which I could contact for more specific information?

Thank you for your help, and I look forward to hearing from you.

Yours faithfully

Katrin Berger

Katrin Berger

2. ***Hinweise:*** *Bei dieser Aufgabe handelt es sich um eine klassische einsträngige Erörterung. Sie sollen sich auseinander setzen mit dem Einfluss Gleichaltriger auf Sie und mit dem Problem des Gruppenzwangs. Als Nachtrag erwartet man auch Ihre Stellungnahme zur Frage, ob Sie sich überreden lassen würden, Marihuana auszuprobieren. Der Hauptteil Ihres Textes umfasst also den Einfluss Gleichaltriger auf Sie, das Problem des Gruppenzwangs und Ihre Stellungnahme zum Marihuana-Probieren. Generell ist eine in drei Abschnitte getrennte Diskussion denkbar (siehe Lösungsbeispiel). Der Einfluss Gleichaltriger und das Problem Gruppenzwang lassen sich aber auch miteinander verbunden erörtern, da beides sehr eng zusammenhängt. Entscheiden Sie, welches Vorgehen in Ihrem Fall sinnvoll ist, wenn Sie Ihre Stoffsammlung ordnen. Dann ist auch wichtig zu prüfen, welches Vokabular des logischen Ordnens notwendig ist für mehr Klarheit in der Aussage. Da Ihr Text in großem Maße Ihre persönlichen Anschauungen widerspiegelt, setzen Sie Redewendungen zur Ankündigung Ihrer Meinung ein. Differenzieren Sie dabei möglichst zwischen großer Überzeugtheit (z. B. "I am convinced/I am sure/certainly") und Annahme (z. B. "I suppose/assume"). Abschließend ergänzen Sie die Einleitung und den Schluss. In der Einleitung führen Sie zum Thema des Hauptteils hin, indem Sie ankündigen, womit Sie sich auseinander setzen werden. Ein dazu passender Slogan, ein Motto oder ein Sprichwort lockern auf und erhöhen die Erwartungshaltung. Im Schlussteil bringen Sie Ihre Erörterungsergebnisse noch einmal kurz und knapp auf den Punkt.*

Peer pressure – how far can you escape it?

"No risk – no fun!" is a motto which is quite popular among young people, who persuade one another to take risks, which they would never dare to do on their own. In the following text I will discuss the influence my peers have on me and the problem of peer pressure.

Let me begin with my peers' influence on me. I suppose that nobody can escape the influence of the others when they are a member of a certain group. Naturally, this also applies to me and the other girls and boys in my class. I think I often do what the group expects of me simply because I do not want to be an outsider. Thus, they influence my manner and behaviour, and even my thinking to a certain degree. Moreover, there are a few people in my class who are the leaders and set the tone. I give in to their ideas to a great extent because there is often no point in swimming against the tide. I do what is "in", and follow the set trends in fashion or music, for example, and adjust to their ideas of what life should be like. All in all, however, I believe their influence gradually becomes restricted to minor matters the more grown-up and independent you are. Your personality develops and you increasingly rely on your own initiative. Peer influence loses its importance step by step.

Second, I will discuss the problem of peer pressure. I suppose that peer pressure works most intensively with young people in puberty because their personality is still developing and is not yet very distinct. I believe peer pressure is natural for this age group and can be alright as long as there is no harm done. However, there are limits, among which wearing brand-name clothes is still the lesser of the evils. Peer pressure may easily get out of control when troublemakers have the final word. In this case such pressure may escalate. We all know about bullying at school or gangs with criminal tendencies. To my mind, how far you are affected by such pressure depends a lot on your age and strength of character as well as the support you get from the people around you.

The leaders in my class would probably find it very difficult to persuade me to do something illegal, and neither would they be able to talk me into doing something completely against my principles, like bullying a classmate. Yet, I can understand that it may be hard to stand up to the pressure, even more so when the others are in the majority. You often do not stand a chance on your own and you need parents, teachers and friends at your side who care.

Finally, I would like to comment on whether I could be talked into using marijuana. Well, the first thing that comes to my mind is 'never say never'. Basically, I am against drugs because the risk you take is not worth it. The problem is that soft drugs like marijuana or ecstasy are becoming more and more socially acceptable. Whereas most young people definitely shrink back from hard drugs and cannot be persuaded to use them, their attitude towards soft drugs is more moderate. As a result, the inhibition level as regards a joint or a pill is much lower. Nevertheless, I would not easily be persuaded to use them because there is no such thing as a harmless soft drug. What I personally fear most are situations that get out of control and undermine your willpower, e. g. a high-spirited party atmosphere. Let's hope I will always be able to avoid temptation.

In conclusion, I suppose that you cannot completely escape peer pressure and the influence of your peers, and I think this is no problem as long as there is no harm in it. However, I am against escalating forms of peer pressure. In this respect, I hope I will always find the strength to resist.

> **Besondere Leistungsfeststellung Thüringen 10. Klasse Englisch**
> **Übungsaufgabe 5**

Bokanovsky's Process – a 1932 fiction of cloning?

Despite being written in 1932, Aldous Huxley's science-fiction novel *Brave New World* prophetically predicts human cloning and the manipulation of embryonic development. Tragically, at the turn of the millennium, these predictions, which were far ahead of Huxley's time, are on the brink of becoming reality.

5 The people in Huxley's brave new world are divided into castes. Alphas, the super-intelligent, are at the top of the caste system, Betas are underneath, Deltas and the dwarfed, semi-moron Epsilons are at the bottom, having little social function and operating simply as workers. The author's incredible predictions already begin in the first chapter, where the Director of the Central London
10 Hatchery and Conditioning Centre is explaining Bokanovsky's Process to future employees.

After fertilization, so the reader learns, it is determined where the fertilized eggs will fit in the caste system. Whereas the Alphas and Betas remain bottled in the incubators, the Deltas and Epsilons are taken out after thirty-six hours to undergo
15 Bokanovsky's Process. The process aims at budding: the dividing of the fertilized egg so that one egg divides into ninety-six identical eggs (at maximum) which will grow into ninety-six perfectly formed embryos later. To make the eggs bud they are exposed to a series of developmental arrests. First the eggs undergo hard X-ray, to which they paradoxically respond by budding. After two
20 days they are chilled, and the buds in their turn bud again. Finally, they are dosed with alcohol and again they respond by budding. Thereafter, as any further arrest would be fatal, they are left to develop in peace and returned to the bottles, their incubators.

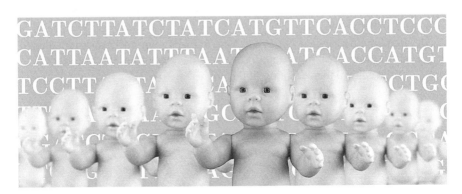

The reader then learns about the ripening process, during which the bottled
25 embryos are transported on conveyor belts, as on an assembly line, which move
slowly over tiers of racks. Once the foetuses have lost their tails they are specially
conditioned for their future role. There is a conditioning routine for every function
in society, from the Alpha-Plus scientist to the Beta-Minus technician to the
Epsilon sewage worker. Across the whole spectrum of embryonic manipulation
30 (e. g. heat conditioning, immunisation against tropical diseases, toleration of
special chemicals or constant rotation), oxygen supply is used for conditioning
the intellect of the castes. Whereas the Alphas are given extra doses of oxygen to
stimulate their intellectual capacity – the normal quantum suffices for the Betas –,
the Deltas and Epsilons are given a short oxygen supply. The shorter the oxygen
35 supply, the more the brain and the skeleton are affected. At 70 % of the normal
oxygen supply, so the reader is told, you get dwarfed Epsilons.
After two-hundred and sixty-seven days of continuous travelling and individualized conditioning, the babies are decanted – the equivalent of birth –, resulting in
thousands and thousands of virtually identical babies, all conditioned for a specific
40 lifestyle.
The second chapter takes the reader to the Infant Nurseries, the Neo-Pavlovian
Conditioning Rooms, where psychological conditioning of the children is under-
taken. Hypnopaedia and sleep-teaching, being the lesser of the evils, are used
to ...
45 However, read about the incredible methods of infant manipulation for your-
selves and reflect on Huxley's (not so) brave new world on your own.

A **Working on the text:**
   Reading comprehension and organizing information   (25 BE)

1. Scan the text for the different castes in Huxley's *Brave New World* and
   use the information to compare them briefly and in an organized way.
   Include aspects such as social position, function in society and intel-
   lect/qualities.

2. Read the passages about *Brave New World's* reproduction system and
   show briefly and in an appropriate way the steps from the fertilization
   of the eggs to the decanting of the babies.

B   Creative writing   (25 BE)

Choose one of the following tasks. Write a text of at least 200 words.

1. An imaginary letter to Aldous Huxley
   Aldous Huxley has been dead for about 40 years, but if he could, he
   would certainly be interested in the state of science and technology today. Write an imaginary letter to him, telling him about recent developments in science and technology e. g. genetic engineering, cloning etc.

2. Unfeasible! Incredible!
   Write a short story, either science-fiction or fantasy, about something
   which seems unfeasible or incredible by present-day standards.

Vocabulary

(to) affect	beeinträchtigen	*hatchery*	Brut-
arrest of	Hemmung der	*incredible*	unglaublich
development	Entwicklung	*incubator*	Brutkasten
assembly line	Fließband	*infant*	Kleinkind
brain	Gehirn	*(to) operate*	arbeiten
brink	Rand	*oxygen*	Sauerstoff
(to) bud	knospen, sprossen	*(to) predict/*	vorhersagen/Vorher-
(to) chill	abkühlen	*prediction*	sage
(to) condition	in einen gewünschten	*quantum*	Menge
	Zustand bringen	*rack*	Regal
continuous	ununterbrochen	*(to) respond*	reagieren
conveyor belt	Transportband	*ripening*	Reifungs-
(to) decant	vorsichtig abgießen	*semi-moron*	halb schwachsinnig
(to) dose	verabreichen	*sewage*	Abwasser
dwarfed	zwergenhaft	*skeleton*	Skellet
equivalent	Entsprechung	*(to) suffice*	genügen
(to be) exposed	(etwas) ausgesetzt sein	*supply*	Versorgung
		tier	Reihe, Lage
fatal	tödlich	*toleration*	Widerstandsfähigkeit
fertilize/	befruchten/	*unfeasible*	unausführbar,
fertilization	Befruchtung		nicht machbar

Lösungen

A Working on the text

1. *Hinweise: Sie sollen den Text nach Informationen zum Kastensystem in Huxleys „Schöne Neue Welt" suchend lesen und die gefundenen Informationen nutzen, um einen Vergleich der Kasten in knapper und logisch geordneter Weise zu erstellen. Überfliegen Sie zunächst den Text und markieren Sie alle zutreffenden Textaussagen. Dann lesen Sie die markierten Textstellen genauer und ordnen sie den vorgeschlagenen Aspekten (gesellschaftliche Stellung, Aufgabe in der Gesellschaft, Intelligenz/Eigenschaften) zu. Denkbar wäre noch ggf. ein vierter Aspekt: Sauerstoffmanipulation für den gewünschten Intelligenzgrad. Nicht immer werden zu allen Kasten direkte Aussagen zu den einzelnen Aspekten gemacht, d. h. Sie müssen hier z. T. auch interpretierend vorgehen: zwischen den Zeilen lesen, Rückschlüsse ziehen auf der Basis der direkten Aussagen und Verallgemeinerungen vornehmen.*

Schlüsseltextstellen:

– *Social position:*
  "*Alphas, the super-intelligent, are at the <u>top of the caste system</u>, <u>Betas are underneath</u>, <u>Deltas</u> and the dwarfed, semi-moron <u>Epsilons</u> are <u>at the bottom</u>, ...*" *(ll. 5–7)*

– *Function in society:*
  "*<u>Alphas</u>, the <u>super-intelligent</u>, ... (ll. 5/6)*
  "*There is a conditioning routine for every function in society, from the <u>Alpha-Plus scientist</u> to the <u>Beta-Minus technician</u> to the <u>Epsilon sewage worker</u>.*" *(ll. 27–29)*
  "*... Deltas and the <u>dwarfed, semi-moron</u> Epsilons are at the bottom, having little social function and operating simply as workers ...*" *(ll. 6–8)*

– *Intellect/qualities:*
  "*<u>Alphas</u>, the <u>super-intelligent</u>, are the ...*" *(ll. 5/6)*
  "*... and the <u>dwarfed, semi-moron</u> Epsilons are ...*" *(l. 7)*

– *Oxygen conditioning to achieve the required intellectual level:*
  "*Whereas the <u>Alphas</u> are given <u>extra doses</u> of oxygen to stimulate their intellectual capacity – the <u>normal quantum</u> suffices for the <u>Betas</u>-, the <u>Deltas and Epsilons</u> are given a <u>short oxygen supply</u>. <u>The shorter the oxygen supply, the more the brain and the skeleton are affected</u>. <u>At 70 % of the normal oxygen supply</u>, so the reader is told, you get <u>dwarfed Epsilons</u>.*" *(ll. 32–36)*

Darstellungsform:

Vergleiche lassen sich in der Regel sehr effektiv in tabellarischer Form ausführen. Beschriften Sie die Zeilen und Spalten mit den vier Kasten bzw. den drei (oder vier) Aspekten. Mitunter ist eine eindeutige Unterscheidung zwischen Deltas und Epsilons nicht möglich. Dann verzichten Sie in der betreffenden Spalte auf den Trennungsstrich.

Caste	Social position	Function in society	Intellect/ qualities	Oxygen conditioning to achieve the required intellectual level
Alpha	the top of the caste system	brain workers, whose functions in society require great intellect, e. g. scientists	super-intelligent	extra doses
Beta	underneath the Alphas	white- and blue-collar workers, whose functions require average intellect, e. g. technicians	of normal intelligence	normal quantum
Delta	at the bottom of the caste system	little social function, simple workers, whose jobs do not require brains Epsilons: e. g. sewage workers	less intelligent	short oxygen supply
Epsilon			dwarfed semi-moron	70 % of normal oxygen

2. **Hinweise:** *Sie sollen das Fortpflanzungssystem in „Schöne neue Welt" genauer untersuchen und dessen Schritte von der Befruchtung des Eis bis zur „Abschöpfung" der Babys in knapper und geeigneter Weise darstellen. Lesen Sie die entsprechenden Abschnitte genau und markieren Sie die Textstellen. Günstig ist bereits beim Markieren für die Alphas und Betas eine Farbe zu verwenden und für die Deltas und Epsilons eine andere, da Sie später beim Notieren diese Unterscheidung benötigen. Erst ab dem Reifungsprozess wird eine Differenzierung zwischen allen vier Kasten notwendig. Ordnen Sie Ihren Markierungen eine Schrittbezeichnung zu: "Fertilization of the eggs, Determination where fertilized eggs will fit into the caste system, Intellectual conditioning of the foetuses during the ripening process and the decanting of the babies". Bei Bokanovskys Prozess finden Sie ebenfalls geeignete Schrittbezeichnungen, z. B. "first step, second step, final step".*

Schlüsseltextstellen:

"After fertilization, so the reader learns, it is determined where the fertilized eggs will fit in the caste system. Whereas the Alphas and Betas remain bottled in the incubators, the Deltas and Epsilons are taken out after thirty-six hours to undergo Bokanovsky's Process." (ll. 12–15)

"To make the eggs bud they are exposed to a series of developmental arrests. First the eggs undergo hard X-ray, to which they paradoxically respond by budding. After two days they are chilled, and the buds in their turn bud again. Finally, they are dosed with alcohol and again they respond by budding. Thereafter, as any further arrest would be fatal, they are left to develop in peace and returned to the bottles, their incubators." (ll. 17–24)

"The reader then learns about the ripening process, ... Once the foetuses have lost their tails they are specially conditioned for their future role ... Across the whole spectrum of embryonic manipulation (e. g. heat conditioning, immunisation against tropical diseases, toleration of special chemicals or constant rotation), oxygen supply is used for conditioning the intellect of the castes. Whereas the Alphas are given extra doses of oxygen to stimulate their intellectual capacity – the normal quantum suffices for the Betas –, the Deltas and Epsilons are given a short oxygen supply. The shorter the oxygen supply, the more the brain and the skeleton are affected. At 70 % of the normal oxygen supply, so the reader is told, you get dwarfed Epsilons. (ll. 24–36)

"After two-hundred and sixty-seven days of continuous travelling and individualized conditioning, the babies are decanted – the equivalent of birth, ..." (ll. 37/38)

Darstellungsform:

Da der Ablauf von Prozessen darzustellen ist, eignet sich ein Prozess- oder Flussdiagramm für das übersichtliche Notieren der einzelnen Schritte. Überlegen Sie anfangs, welche Schrittbezeichnungen für alle Kasten gleich sind (Befruchtung, Kastenzuordnung, Intellektmanipulation, „Abschöpfung"). Dann erarbeiten Sie die notwendigen Differenzierungen in der Darstellung. Alphas und Betas werden zunächst gleich behandelt, und Deltas und Epsilons durchlaufen gemeinsam Bokanovskys Prozess, sodass hier beim Notieren zunächst nur zwischen den zwei Kastengruppen zu unterscheiden ist. Später bei der Intellektmanipulation ist ein Differenzieren zwischen allen vier Kasten erforderlich. Grenzen Sie beim Notieren die Kasten klar voneinander ab und nutzen Sie Pfeile für das Verdeutlichen der Abfolge.

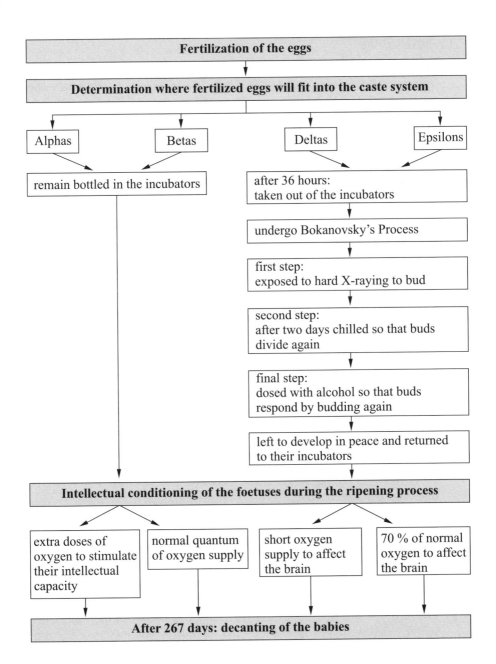

B Creative writing

1. *Hinweise: Ziel dieser Schreibaufgabe ist es, einen fiktiven Brief an Aldous Huxley, den Autor des Romans* Brave New World, *zu schreiben. Dabei sollen Sie den vor über 40 Jahren verstorbenen Autor über jüngere Entwicklungen auf dem Gebiet von Wissenschaft und Technik informieren. Vorgeschlagen werden Ihnen dazu das weite Feld der Gentechnik und das Klonen. Beide Themen haben den Autor schon vor über 70 Jahren stark beschäftigt, auch wenn zu jener Zeit die Begriffe an sich unbekannt waren. Diese Themen zu bearbeiten bedeutet, dass man zahlreiche Berührungspunkte zum Roman findet und so den Brief etwas persönlicher halten kann. Der Lesetext bietet diesbezüglich ausreichend Ansatzpunkte. Natürlich steht es Ihnen frei, auf andere wissenschaftliche Entwicklungen einzugehen. Um den Brief nicht wie einen informierenden Artikel wirken zu lassen, ist es angebracht, den Autor z. B. anzusprechen, zu fragen, um seine Meinung zu bitten. Im Beispielbrief wird auch die Hochachtung vor seinem Lebenswerk zum Ausdruck gebracht. Beachten Sie beim Verfassen die typischen äußeren Merkmale eines persönlichen Schreibens: z. B. Absender, Datum, Anrede, Grußformel am Schluss. Stilistisch sind eine weniger förmliche oder ungefärbte Stilebene angebracht. Für ein ansprechendes Ergebnis sollten Sie versuchen, die geforderte Mindestwortzahl von 200 um einiges zu überschreiten.*

Alexanderstr. 12
07548 Gera
Germany
17th September 2003

Dear Mr Huxley,

Although you have been dead for quite a long time I'm writing to tell you about recent developments in cloning because I'm sure that you would be interested if you were alive.

About 70 years after you wrote *Brave New World*, most of your prophecies have come true or are on the brink of becoming reality. Just as you predicted, scientists can now produce humans outside of the womb, and we are only a hair's breadth away from human cloning. Therefore, let me express my deep respect for your great foresight and your urgent warnings, which are now of interest more than ever.

I believe you still lived to see the first animal cloned when they duplicated simple tadpoles from tadpole cells. And meanwhile you may have heard of Molly, the Scottish sheep that was cloned in 1996. To date, I think several species of mammal have been successfully cloned, but numerous attempts with primates have failed so far. However, scientists claim that cloning humans is entirely possible.

In January this year, reports from the Raelians, a religious cult, claimed that the first human clones had been born. The whole world held their breath. But, like most people, I'm sceptical about the truth of this claim because the Raelians won't allow genetic testing to confirm that the infants are indeed clones.

Anyway, to my mind such charlatan stories show the need to pass laws that cover the entire spectrum of reproductive genetics. In November 2002, the United Nations tried to adopt an international convention banning reproductive human cloning, but no consensus was reached. Some countries already have this legislation, and others even want to ban therapeutic cloning.

However, I suppose appropriate legislation is like walking on a tightrope. It's not simply a black and white issue, because there's a tremendous difference between reproductive and therapeutic cloning. I'm not so sure about a ban on therapeutic cloning because scientists are actually not copying embryos. What they do is take the genetic material from a cell in an adult body and fuse it with an empty egg cell. Thus, one day scientists could mine these embryonic stem cells for special cells to be used in medical treatment. New nerve cells could be transplanted into sufferers of Parkinson's and Alzheimer's disease. New heart muscle could repair damaged hearts. With therapeutic cloning, a leukaemia patient could even get the right bone marrow by using his/her own cells. On the other hand, it can't be denied that therapeutic cloning interferes with Creation and the natural selection of man. In this respect, I wonder what you think of this special form of cloning and if you would support it because of the benefit that could be derived from it.

The question we are posed with in our day and age is where to draw the line. As you impressively showed in your book, cloning can easily be detrimental to mankind despite its useful possibilities. If we allow cloning to occur freely, we will travel further down the path you urgently warned us against taking. Let's hope all the governments in the world will put firm regulations on cloning and thus determine what path man will eventually take.

With this in mind, I pay my deepest respects to your life's work.

Yours,

Steven Burghardt

Steven Burghardt

2. **Hinweise:** *Gegenstand dieser Schreibaufgabe ist das Erzählen einer Kurz-geschichte aus der Science-Fiction- oder Fantasiewelt. Thema der Erzählung soll etwas für unsere heutige Zeit Unmachbares oder Unglaubliches sein. Suchen Sie zunächst nach einem geeigneten Stoff. Vielleicht gibt etwas der-zeit Unmögliches, von dem Sie persönlich wünschen, es wäre machbar. Oder aber Sie verleihen Befürchtungen, die Sie für die Zukunft haben, den Anschein der Realität. Ist das Sujet gefunden, betten Sie den Gegenstand in eine Hand-lung und lassen Ihren Helden oder Ihre Heldin agieren. Schmücken Sie die Handlung mit Science-Fiction oder Fantasie-Details aus. Wenn sinnvoll, er-zählen Sie die Geschichte auf ein überraschendes Ende hin für mehr Span-nung. Ein offenes Ende wäre eine andere Möglichkeit.*

Sujet der nachfolgenden Beispielgeschichte ist die vollständige Umwandlung des äußeren Erscheinungsbildes eines Menschen. Die Handlung darum ist die Rückreise Julias nach der Umwandlungsoperation und die Identitätsver-wechslung bei Ankunft. Die Geschichte wird auf die Pointe hin erzählt, dass eine Neptun-Spionin mit Julias früherem Erscheinungsbild entwischen kann. Die Heldin Julia „agiert" vorwiegend reflektierend, es werden nur wenige notwendige Aktivitäten der Heldin erwähnt, um den Fortgang der Handlung zu ermöglichen. In einer Rückblende erfährt der Leser, wie Julia sich für Ihr neues Äußeres entscheidet. Verschiedene Details werden eingesetzt, um zeit-liches Versetzen in die Zukunft zu unterstützen. Als Erzählperspektive wird das personale Erzählen gewählt. Durch innere Monologe, Selbstgespräche und erlebte, halbdirekte Rede kann der Leser sich in das Geschehen einfühlen.

Beauty is no defence in law

Incredible. Julia looked like a completely different woman. They had done wonders for her at Campbell's Beauty and Rejuvenation Centre. Every single feature of her looks, even the smallest details were to perfection. Absolutely nothing in her appearance was a reminder of the plain middle-aged woman she had been only yesterday. In an hour's time Julia would be back home. Her husband had promised to meet her. She had had the good sense to send him her new image over the telepathic transmitter. As a matter of fact, she would soon have to do this to everyone she knew her if she wanted to be re-recognized.

Julia strolled up and down the air taxi platform. With every step she felt the appreciative eyes of the men on her and she bathed in this pool of admiration with relish. Her air taxi to Morecambe seemed to be fully booked today. Odd! Usually there would only be a few people. Maybe some of the male tra-vellers would change to sea taxi at Morecambe and continue to NCI5 Island, where the Neptune Counter-Intelligence Unit had its headquarters. The feelings-conditioned cabin lulled her into a euphoric sense of uniqueness.

How difficult everything had seemed at first! 112 different shades of hair colouring, 67 forms of nose, eyes from seductive, catlike ones to big, wide, shining ones. That questionnaire with more than 500 beauty items to decide upon still made her head spin. The image style sheets had been like the answer to a prayer. Within an hour Julia had worked through the images she had in mind for herself. Her choice narrowed down to three and the die was cast when the plastic surgeon pointed out the one he had never applied to any woman before. Would her new ravishing beauty give their marriage back the fire she had been longing for since their seventieth wedding anniversary?

The loudspeakers announced their arrival. Julia pressed the luggage button to have her belongings conveyed to her home and waited for confirmation. When it didn't come, she pressed the button again. Strangely enough the green light didn't show. System failure hardly ever occurred these days. Maybe a little fuse in her service box had gone. On her way out she would inquire whether her luggage call had been received. Now it was only a question of a few minutes till she would see her husband's reaction to her miraculous change. He had already telepathed that he was waiting for her outside the gates.

At the check-out she removed the protective cover from the identity chip in her ear lobe and wanted to walk on when suddenly something invisible stopped her feet from moving and she nearly fell over. It took her some seconds to understand what was happening. It was the infamous electronic shackles she had heard of but never seen in operation. Then she was surrounded by men, the same men, she now realized, who had been on the platform. "Soniara Nertukio, we arrest you on the grounds of espionage for the Neptunian government ..." "This is a misunderstanding! You've mistaken my identity. I'm not ..." The cautioning interrupted her. Then they explained, "Our sources have reported that you sought to change your image at Campbell's Beauty and Rejuvenation Centre, but were turned back because they had the feeling that something fishy was going on. Now that the check-out control signalled you as an unidentified object we have reason to believe ..." Julia felt like she was in a bad spy movie from the ancient Hollywood days. The other travellers pushed impatiently through the crowd. Then a plain middle-aged woman in the crowd caught Julia's eye. She gaped. No! Anything but that! Her mind tried to digest the incredible. "There ..." The words stuck in her throat. Speechlessly she watched the plain woman leave, the woman who was the exact image of her former self.

Besondere Leistungsfeststellung Thüringen 10. Klasse Englisch	
Übungsaufgabe 6	

Tahoe Extreme Sports Camp – Go Extreme All Day!

Tahoe Extreme Sports Camp is a new concept in Summer Camp for kids of all athletic abilities and skill levels from ages 7 through 18. At *www.800procamp.com*, the camp's homepage, you will see that the camp supplies practically everything for a breath-taking holiday, so all young campers need is a keen appetite for
5 adventure and thrills and a desire to try new things and meet new people.
Tahoe Extreme Sports Camp is located in Squaw Valley, Lake Tahoe, California – one of the most picturesque settings in the world. The Lake is divided in half by the California-Nevada State line. The camp is on the northwest end of the Lake, about 40 miles from Reno and a three and a half hour drive from San
10 Francisco.
Activities there are guaranteed "to knock your socks off", as they claim. And they are extreme indeed: reverse bungee, glider flights, skateboard park, wakeboard, tubing, go-kart racing, white water rafting, extreme mountain biking, rock climbing, kayaking, mountain scooter, off road hummer rides or speedboat rides
15 and many more will provide you with all the kicks you need. Naturally, the safety of the campers is excellently provided for with top of the line equipment, qualified staff and the enforcement of strict safety rules. Moreover, most activities are based more on the feeling of risk rather than actual risk. "All our activities are very high on adrenaline and very low on risk," they promise.

20 During their stay the campers live at Squaw Valley Academy, a dorm-style facility with four to six kids per room with their own bathroom. There is 24 hour super- vision there, and the counsellors are always present to tend to the campers' needs. Breakfast and dinner are
25 served family-style in the dining room and lunch is supplied picnic-style on-the-go. Every night the kids choose their activities for the next day. Activities are picked nightly so that as kids make new friends they can choose to be together for the day. As campers
30 come from all over the world and use the camp to improve their English, it is more than just a summer camp, but a cultural experience as well.

Routine	
7:30	Wake-Up
8:00	Breakfast
9:00	Activities
12:00	Lunch
1:00	Activities
6:00	Dinner
7:00	Evening activity
9:00	Back to the dorm
9:30	Lights out

Sessions at the Extreme Sports Camp are usually 7 days long from Sunday to Saturday, fees being $ 1,495 a week.

35 The Camp hires all its counsellors from Camp America, an agency specialized in finding qualified staff for summer work experience. Camp America does the preliminary interviews. Then Tahoe Camp personnel managers go to England to meet and handpick the ones suitable for their programme. Applicants for a counsellor's position apply to Camp America six months in advance. They must be
40 18 or over by 1 June of the year to come and have previous experience working with children. They should be athletic, great role models and First Aid and CPR certified. Counsellors in charge of watersports must also have lifeguard certifications. All applicants are pre-screened and go through extensive background checks. Any individuals with a criminal record will not be accepted. From appli-
45 cants whose native tongue is other than English, a good command of the English language is required.

A Working on the text:
Reading comprehension and organizing information (25 BE)

1. Create a one-page leaflet about Tahoe Extreme Sports Camp with the aim of attracting kids and teenagers to this camp and providing them with information about it. Use any information from the text you think appropriate. Pay attention to the style, e. g. informal and personal, striking and provocative. Try to work on a suitable layout.

2. Show briefly and in an organized way how you personally meet the requirements to apply for the position of counsellor at Tahoe Extreme Sports Camp. Include any conclusions you would draw if you wanted to apply there in the future.

B Creative writing (25 BE)

Choose one of the following tasks. Write a text of at least 200 words.

1. Applying for the position of counsellor at Tahoe Extreme Sports Camp
   Imagine you will be 18 by June 1, 200...* and are interested in working as a counsellor at Tahoe Extreme Sports Camp. Write a letter of application to Camp America, the agency where they hire their staff from. Add your CV in tabular form.

   postal address: e-mail address:
   Camp America   enquiries@campamerica.co.uk
   37A Queen's Gate
   London
   SW7 5HR
   Great Britain
   * (Jahr des folgenden Sommers)

2. No Risk – No Fun
   What do you think of this motto? How far does going extreme appeal to you personally?

Vocabulary

ability	Fähigkeit	*on-the-go*	auf Achse
(in) advance	vorher, (im) Voraus	*(to) pick*	auswählen
(to) appeal	reizen, Anklang finden	*picturesque*	malerisch
breath-taking	atemberaubend	*preliminary*	vorausgehend
certified	bescheinigt	*pre-screened*	vorausgewählt
charge (in ~ of)	verantwortlich	*previous*	vorherige
command	Beherrschung	*rafting (white*	Wildwasserfahrten
counsellor	Gruppenleiter	*water ~)*	
CPR (= cardio-	Wiederbelebungs-	*require*	erwarten
pulmonary	technik für Herz- und	*reverse*	umgekehrt
resuscitation)	Lungenfunktion	*role model*	Vorbild
criminal record	polizeilich erfasste	*scooter*	Roller
	Straftat	*session*	Durchgang
desire	Bedürfnis, Wunsch	*setting*	Lage, Gegend
dorm-style	wohnheimartig	*skill*	Fertigkeit
enforcement	Durchsetzung	*staff*	Personal
facility	Einrichtung	*strict*	streng
fee	Gebühr, Kosten	*supervision*	Beaufsichtigung
glider	Segelflugzeug	*(to) supply*	versorgen
(to) go extreme	zum Äußersten gehen	*thrill*	Nervenkitzel
(to) hire	ein-, anstellen	*tubing*	Wassersport, bei dem
keen	versessen		der Sportler auf einem
(to) knock your	umhauen		luftgefüllten Schlauch
socks off (slang)			sitzt
off road		*wakeboard*	dem Wasserski ähnlich,
hummer ride	Jeep-Geländefahrten		jedoch mit einem Brett
			unter den Füßen

Lösungen

A Working on the text

1. *Hinweise: Hier wird von Ihnen eine interessante Art der Informationsverarbeitung erwartet, die in besonderem Maße Ansprüche an Ihre Kreativität stellt. Aufgabe ist, einen einseitigen Prospekt für das Tahoe Extremsport-Camp zu erstellen mit dem Ziel, Kinder und Jugendliche auf das Camp aufmerksam zu machen und sie darüber zu informieren. Für den erforderlichen Prospekttext sollen Sie nach Ihrer Meinung geeignete Informationen aus dem Lesetext entnehmen. Die Auswahl der Informationen unterliegt natürlich bestimmten Zwecken: das Interesse der Kinder und Jugendlichen wecken und sie ggf. zu einem Camp-Aufenthalt animieren, aber auch das sachliche Informieren über einen solchen Ferienaufenthalt. Weiterhin soll der Stil diesen Zwecken dienen und adressatengerecht ungezwungen und persönlich, aber auch schlagfertig und herausfordernd sein. Ein geeignetes Layout ist zu finden. Mögliche Lesestrategie können sein: ein Search-Reading des Textes für das gezielte Auffinden von werbewirksamen Textaussagen, die Ihnen später beim Formulieren von Prospekt-Slogans dienlich sein können und ein detailliertes Lesen aller zum Camp und zum Camp-Aufenthalt gehörigen Aussagen (Kontakt, Lage, Teilnehmer, Extremsportaktivitäten, Aufenthalt etc.). Die Schwierigkeit bei Letzterem besteht im Aussortieren der vielen nützlichen, aber für Kinder und Jugendliche nicht unbedingt erwähnenswerten Aussagen.*

Schlüsseltextstellen:

slogans:

"Tahoe Extreme Sports Camp – <u>Go Extreme All Day!</u>" (l. 0)

"At www.800procamp.com, the camp's homepage you will see that the camp supplies <u>practically everything for a breath-taking holiday</u>, so all young campers need is <u>a keen appetite for adventure and thrills and a desire to try new things</u> and meet new people." (ll. 2–5)

"Activities there are guaranteed '<u>to knock your socks off</u>', as they claim. And they are extreme <u>indeed:</u> ..." (ll. 11/12)

"... reverse bungee, glider flights, skateboard park, wakeboard, tubing, go-kart racing, white water rafting, extreme mountain biking, rock climbing, kayaking, mountain scooter, off road hummer rides or speedboat rides and many more <u>will provide you with all the kicks you need</u>." (ll. 12–15)

"Naturally, the <u>safety</u> of the campers is <u>excellently provided for</u> with <u>top of the line equipment</u>, qualified staff and the enforcement of strict safety rules. Moreover, most activities are based more on the feeling of risk rather than actual risk. '<u>All our activities are very high on adrenaline and very low on risk</u>' they promise." (ll. 15–19)

camp/stay at the camp:

– *contact:*
"At www.800procamp.com, the camp's homepage you will see ..."
(ll. 2/3)

– *location:*
"Tahoe Extreme Sports Camp is located in Squaw Valley, Lake Tahoe, California – one of the most picturesque settings in the world. The Lake is divided in half by the California-Nevada State line. The camp is on the northwest end of the Lake, about 40 miles from Reno and a three and a half hour drive from San Francisco." (ll. 5–10)

– *campers:*
"Tahoe Extreme Sports Camp is a new concept in Summer Camp for kids of all athletic abilities and skill levels from ages 7 through 18." (ll. 1/2)

– *extreme sports activities:*
"... reverse bungee, glider flights, skateboard park, wakeboard, tubing, go-kart racing, white water rafting, extreme mountain biking, rock climbing, kayaking, mountain scooter, off road hummer rides or speedboat rides and many more will provide you with all the kicks you need." (ll. 12–15)

– *stay:*
"During their stay the campers live at Squaw Valley Academy, a dorm-style facility with four to six kids per room with their own bathroom." (ll. 20–22)
"Sessions at the Extreme Sports Camp are usually 7 days long from Sunday to Saturday, fees being $1,495 a week." (ll. 34/35)
"Routine 7:30 Wake-Up, 8:00 Breakfast, 9:00 Activities, 12:00 Lunch, 1:00 Activities, 6:00 Dinner, 7:00 Evening activity, 9:00 Back to the dorm, 9:30 Lights out" (ll. 20–30)

Darstellungsform:

Als Vorgabe ist von einem einseitigen Prospekt auszugehen. Für das Layout gibt es vielfältigste Möglichkeiten, und Ihrer Fantasie sind keine Grenzen gesetzt. Sinnvoll ist in jedem Fall, die Prospekttexte etwas zu ordnen und ggf. Slogans, die die Aufmerksamkeit wecken sollen, räumlich etwas abzugrenzen von den Sachinformationen. Dabei können Sie z. B. mit unterschiedlichen Schriftgrößen und Farben operieren: die große Schriftart/die auffällige Farbe für das Aufmerksammachen. Die Sachaussagen können kleiner/unauffälliger abgesetzt werden, denn ist wirkliches Interesse geweckt, wird dann auch weitergelesen. Die Sachaussagen ihrerseits sollten wiederum nach bestimmten Teilaspekten geordnet werden: Kontakt, Lage, Teilnehmer, Extremsportaktivitäten, Aufenthalt etc. Teilüberschriften, die kurz ankündigen, was folgt, erhöhen die Übersichtlichkeit und Lesbarkeit. Legen Sie sich auf eine bestimmte Formulierungsart fest und wenden Sie diese Diktion bei allen Teilüberschriften an. Im Lösungsbeispiel kommt die indirekte Frage als Diktion zur Anwendung ("Who can come:", "Where you live:", "Where to find us:", ...). Eine andere Diktion ist z. B. das Nominalisieren ("Participants:", "Accommodation:", "Location:" ...), welches aber sehr förmlich wirkt und daher mehr für eine Erwachsenenzielgruppe geeignet ist. Liegen die Prospekttexte fest, überlegen Sie, mit welchen einfachen Illustrationen die Aussage unterstützt werden kann (Bildmaterial, wie es im Lösungsbeispiel verwendet wurde, steht Ihnen in einer Prüfungssituation in der Regel nicht zur Verfügung). Mit Bildunterschriften können Sie noch einmal ansprechen ("Ever tried ...?") oder provozieren ("Nothing for scaredy cats!"). Zum Schluss finden Sie noch einen ungewöhnlichen/provozierenden Slogan, der als Überschrift dienen kann, z. B. "Go extreme all day!, No risk – no fun!, All you ever wanted, but never dared!"

Go Extreme All Day!

Interested in activities that knock your socks off?

Visit us at **www.800procamp.com** and find out about more than 20 different extreme sports you can do in our camp.

Then
Tahoe Extreme Sports Camp
is the right thing for you.

What we offer: Masses of fun, high on adrenaline. Guaranteed!

All you need: a keen appetite for adventure and thrills and a desire to try new things.

Who can come:
- kids and teenagers of all athletic abilities and skill levels
- from ages 7 through 18

What a day in the camp is like:

Nothing for scaredy cats!

7:30	Wake-Up
8:00	Breakfast
9:00	Activities
12:00	Lunch
1:00	Activities
6:00	Dinner
7:00	Evening activity
9:00	Back to the dorm
9:30	Lights out

Where to find us:

- in Squaw Valley, Lake Tahoe, California
- on the northwest end of the Lake
- about 40 miles from Reno
- a three and a half hour drive from San Francisco

Where you live:

- at Squaw Valley Academy
- a dorm-style facility
- four to six kids per room
- own bathroom

How long sessions are:

- 7 days
- from Sunday to Saturday

2. **Hinweise:** *In dieser Aufgabe geht es um das Umwälzen von Informationen auf die eigene Person. Sie sollen kurz und übersichtlich zeigen, wie Sie persönlich die Voraussetzungen und Anforderungen erfüllen, die an einen Bewerber als Gruppenleiter im Tahoe Extremsport-Camp gestellt werden. Außerdem sind Schlussfolgerungen einzubeziehen, zu welchen Sie kommen würden, wenn Sie sich dort irgendwann in der Zukunft bewerben wollten. Lesen Sie zunächst den entsprechenden Abschnitt sehr genau und markieren Sie alle Voraussetzungen und Anforderungen. Diese listen Sie dann beim Notieren auf und stellen gegenüber, welche davon Sie erfüllen bzw. nicht erfüllen. In einem dritten Schritt schlussfolgern Sie, welche unerfüllten Bedingungen/ Anforderungen Sie durch welche Maßnahmen ggf. später erfüllen können.*

Schlüsseltextstellen:

"Applicants for a counsellor's position apply to Camp America six months in advance. They must <u>be 18 or over by 1 June of the year to come</u> and have <u>previous experience working with children</u>. They should <u>be athletic, great role models</u> and <u>First Aid and CPR certified</u>. Counsellors in charge of watersports must also have <u>lifeguard certifications</u>. All applicants are pre-screened and go through extensive background checks. Any individuals with a <u>criminal record</u> will not be accepted. From applicants whose native tongue is other than English, a <u>good command of the English language</u> is required. (ll. 38–46)

Darstellungsform:
Eine tabellarische Übersicht bietet sich hier an. In der linken Spalte listen Sie die Anforderungen untereinander auf. Die nächste Spalte sagt aus, ob Sie diese Voraussetzungen/Anforderungen erfüllen oder nicht. Das kann über ein Ja-/Nein-Prinzip erfolgen und Sie haken bzw. kreuzen entsprechend an. (Im Englischen wird der Haken als ein Ja gewertet und das Kreuz als ein Nein.) In einer dritten Spalte vermerken Sie Ihre Schlussfolgerungen knapp.

Requirements	Fulfilled / met by me		Conclusions
	yes	no	
18 or over by 1 June of the year to come		x	wait for another year
previous experience working with children	✓		a job at a German summer camp next summer – good idea
athletic	✓		maybe take up another sport
great role model	✓		
First Aid certified	✓		
CPR certified		x	take a course with the German Red Cross
lifeguard certification		x	need to wait till I'm 18
criminal record		x	
good command of the English language	✓		should improve it further

B Creative writing

1. **Hinweise:** *Thema der Gestaltungsaufgabe ist das Bewerben bei Camp America für eine Tätigkeit im Tahoe Extremsport-Camp. Es ist ein tabellarischer Lebenslauf beizufügen. Es wird erwartet, dass Sie sich in die Situation der Volljährigkeit versetzen. Beachten Sie, dass Sie sich hier um eine Ferientätigkeit bewerben. Berücksichtigen Sie auch inhaltlich, dass Bewerber mindestens 18 Jahre alt sein müssen. Im Text werden Informationen gegeben zu den verschiedenen Anforderungen an den Bewerber. Diese haben Sie in Aufgabe 2 verarbeitet. Nutzen Sie daher Ihre Verarbeitungsergebnisse für ein gezieltes Eingehen auf die Anforderungen. Bringen Sie zum Ausdruck, wie Sie den geforderten Persönlichkeitsmerkmalen (Sportlichkeit, Vorbildfunktion), Erfahrungen (Umgang mit Kindern), beglaubigte Nachweise (Erste Hilfe/CPR) und gute Sprachkenntnisse gerecht werden. Als Anlagen nennen Sie den Lebenslauf, den Erste-Hilfe-Nachweis und zwei Referenzen.*

Bahnhofstraße 2
99427 Gotha
Germany
10 October 2003

Camp America
37A Queen's Gate
London
SW7 5HR
Great Britain

Dear Sir or Madam

I wish to apply for the position of counsellor at Tahoe Extreme Sports Camp for the summer of 2004.

I am very interested in working at Tahoe Extreme Sports Camp because I feel that working with children, especially in sports would suit my leanings. At present I am a pupil at a German grammar school and I am seriously thinking of studying to become a grammar school teacher of PE and English.

I will be 18 on January 22, 2004. I will be leaving school at the end of this academic year and will be taking my A-levels in April next year. I could leave for the USA after June 1.

I have a great interest in different sports, mainly games, water sports and body-building. I have been a member of our school's handball team for seven years and also gained experience instructing younger players. I worked as a helper at our club's handball training camps in both 2002 and 2003. Swimming is another interest of mine. I am thinking of taking my Lifesaver's Certificate as soon as I am 18. In order to develop my strength and stamina I regularly work out at a local fitness club.

I have been learning the English language for seven years and have been doing an intensive course in English for a year and a half now.

I would be very grateful if you were able to consider me for the position of counsellor. Please find enclosed my curriculum vitae, a photocopy of my First Aid Certificate and two references.

I look forward to hearing from you.

Yours faithfully

Georg Geyer

Georg Geyer

Curriculum Vitae

SURNAME:	Geyer
FIRST NAME:	Georg
ADDRESS	Bahnhofstraße 2, 99867 Gotha
TELEPHONE NUMBER	++ 49 (0)3621 / 995244
DATE OF BIRTH:	22 January 1986
PLACE OF BIRTH:	Gotha, Germany
NATIONALITY:	German
DENOMINATION:	Catholic
MARITAL STATUS:	single
PARENTS:	father: Klaus Geyer – computer support specialist
	mother: Marion Geyer, née Müller – teacher
BROTHERS/SISTERS:	one younger brother
EDUCATION:	from 1992 to 1996:
	Löffler-Primary-School
	Langensalzaer Str. 2, 99867 Gotha
	from 1996 to present:
	Arnoldi-Grammar-School
	Eisenacher Str. 5, 99867 Gotha
LANGUAGES:	mother tongue: German
	English: very good knowledge
	French: good knowledge
QUALIFICATIONS:	will be taking my A-levels in April 2004
FURTHER QUALIFICATIONS:	computer skills
	graduation from local music school (guitar)
	First Aid Certificate
	moped driving licence
	will be taking my Lifesaver's Certificate in January 2004
	experiences as handball instructor
HOBBIES:	handball, swimming, body-building, guitar
NAMES OF REFEREES:	Mr Schröder, Gotha Music School, Eckermannstr. 5, 99867 Gotha
	Mrs Busse, teacher and handball instructor at my present school

Gotha, 10 October 2003

Georg Geyer

2. **Hinweise:** *Kein Spaß ohne Risiko! Was halten Sie von diesem Motto? Inwiefern reizt Sie das Bezwingen von Extremen? Diese Aufgabenstellung gibt Ihnen bereits einen möglichen Aufbau Ihres Textes vor. Gliedern Sie Ihren Hauptteil demzufolge in zwei große Abschnitte: Einstellung zum Motto und Reiz des Bezwingens von Extremen. Beantworten Sie beide Teilaspekte möglichst ausführlich. Versuchen Sie Ihre Einstellung zum Motto von unterschiedlichen Blickwinkeln zu beleuchten, z. B. Mut zum Risiko, Leichtsinn, Verabsolutierung des Spaßverständnisses, Sinn/Widersinn/Selbstzweck usw. Geben Sie Gründe für Ihre Meinung an. Der andere Teilaspekt erfordert das Darstellen, inwiefern Sie persönlich zum Bezwingen von Extremen bereit sind. Begründen Sie auch hier. Betten Sie Ihren Hauptteil in Einleitung und Schluss ein, um den Leser zum Thema hinzuführen bzw. um Ihren Text abzurunden.*

No Risk – No Fun?

There have always been people to whom the ultimate adventure appeals more than to the average individual. Nowadays, however, going extreme seems to have won in popularity among young people especially. In the following I will discuss what I think of the "No risk – No fun!" motto and how far going extreme appeals to me.

Let me begin with my attitude towards this motto. As the saying goes, if you play with fire, you must expect to get your fingers burned. I think there is a lot of truth in this proverb. Yet, some young people do not shy at going extreme to get the ultimate kick. Admittedly, modern extreme sports equipment is reasonably safe today, and fortunately, fatal accidents are rare. But an element of danger always remains. Therefore, I think everyone has to take care of themselves and as long as the risk is restricted to a minimum, going extreme is alright. The fact is that if you do sports, no matter how risky, there is always a certain danger of being hurt or injured. However, I do not approve of activities where the risk factor is unacceptably high and safety uncontrollable, such as suburban train-surfing for instance.

Furthermore, to regard risky activities as the only source of real fun is an extremely one-sided attitude in my opinion, and the motto seems to me much too limited. It goes without saying that there are many ways of enjoying yourself and people can derive fun and pleasure from numerous other activities and sports like I do.

Finally, I believe going extreme just for fun without a meaningful goal is like tempting fate. People who are willing to withstand extreme strain for scientific or other reasons, however, deserve our utmost respect. Without them our world would be a bit poorer.

Now let me say how far going extreme appeals to me personally. I am certainly not a couch potato and am active in several fields, but going extreme does not really entice me. In a way, I find it hard to understand that people simply do risky things because of the kick – the burst of adrenaline – they get from it. And I wonder if it is worth it. Of course, I like doing fast sports e. g. down-hill skiing or mountain biking, but I am experienced in them and I do not only do them because of the thrill of speed. Moreover, I try not to mistake carelessness for courage and I shy at doing something with a high risk factor because the price you might pay for overrating your skills may be too high. Anyway, besides the seasonal skiing and biking, I really like ball games. Handball is a favourite of mine. I like playing together with the others and our joint efforts to win make us a committed team. That and the great feeling of being successful as a team is where I derive my fun and kicks from, for example. Finally, I am convinced that my views apply to a great number of teenagers and young people, because extreme freaks are a minority.

In conclusion, in my opinion the "No Risk – No Fun!" motto is an extremely one-sided idea of fun. There are innumerable low-risk activities and sports which you can get a lot of fun and pleasure from. People to whom going extreme is more important than suffering the possible consequences should do extreme sports. I, however, shy at doing them because an element of risk always remains.

**Besondere Leistungsfeststellung Thüringen 10. Klasse Englisch
2003 – Aufgabe 1**

Young drivers live dangerously

Passing your driving test is a reason to celebrate – an important step on the way to becoming an adult that gives you the freedom of being able to use a car. But many young British drivers do not enjoy their new skills for long.
Every year, road accidents cause the deaths of more than 1,000 young people between the ages of 17 and 21. A teenage driver is seven times more likely to be involved in a fatal accident than a 40-year-old. Road accidents are the most common cause of death in the 15–24 age group.

"Cadillac Ranch" in Amarillo, Texas, is the product of Ant Farm, an American group of artists and architects

The Government has decided that something must be done to cut these figures. A new training scheme has now started, with the aim of helping young drivers to use the roads more safely. The scheme is called Pass Plus, and will teach extra skills to young drivers who have already passed their test. They will get training in driving at night, on motorways, in towns and country and in bad weather. The course will cost £90 for six one-hour lessons.
Special attention will be paid to the way those taking the course behave towards other road users, and the way they deal with dangerous situations. There will be no test, but Pass Plus training will have important advantages. Some insurance companies will make insurance cheaper for people who have done the course. At the moment, new drivers often pay over three times more for insurance than older drivers do.
Not everyone is certain that the new scheme will help to cut road deaths among young people. Research has shown that young people usually have good driving skills. The problem is that they do not use them. They drive faster, like powerful cars, and take too many risks. Young men are the most dangerous drivers. One young driver told researchers, "I drive the car nearer the limits than other people and I know where the limits are. My reflexes are a bit better."

It could be difficult to change this kind of over-confidence with extra training. Another problem is that as Pass Plus is voluntary, the most aggressive and dangerous new drivers may not take it. The Government hopes, however, that even
35 these drivers will be attracted by the lower insurance costs.

From: Read On, August 1995, No. 461

A Working on the text

(25 BE)

Solve the tasks, using your own words as far as appropriate.

1. Read the text and list your keywords under the main headings "Statistics" and "Pass Plus".

2. *Imagine you work for the school magazine of a British school.*
   You are asked to create a one-page leaflet for "Pass Plus". Find a convincing layout and the right language to make your fellow-students take part in this new training scheme. Do not forget to find a striking slogan, be personal and provocative. You may use symbols and/or pictures.

B Creative writing

(25 BE)

Choose one of the following tasks. Write a text of at least 200 words.

1. *After the disco you have missed your last bus. A friend wants to give you a lift home in his or her car although he or she has drunk too much.*
   Make up a dialogue between you and your friend in which you argue about the dilemma of drinking and driving.

2. You like the idea of "Pass Plus" and decide to write an application for this course. Address your letter to:
   Pass Plus – young drivers' scheme, 7a Belfield Drive, Cardiff CF2 1UY, Wales, UK

Lösungsvorschläge

A Working on the text

1. *Hinweise: Aufgabe ist es, Stichpunkte unter den Hauptüberschriften „Statistiken" (nachfolgend Teilaufgabe a) und „Pass Plus" (nachfolgend Teilaufgabe b) anzufertigen. Darunter ist zu verstehen, dass Sie möglichst alle wichtigen Aussagen, die im Text zu beidem gemacht werden, stichpunktartig und entsprechend geordnet notieren. Lesen Sie zunächst die betreffenden Textstellen genau und markieren Sie alle Aussagen geordnet nach Teilaufgabe a und b.*
Teilaufgabe a: Im Text werden lediglich drei statistische Angaben gemacht, die gleichrangig sind und sich so untereinander anordnen lassen.
Teilaufgabe b: Lesen Sie Ihre Textmarkierungen noch einmal sehr sorgfältig. Sortieren Sie und finden Sie geeignete Teilüberschriften, z. B. Initiator, Zielgruppe, Ziel, Methode, Kursinhalt, Gebühren, Vorteile für Kursteilnehmer, Nachteile.

Schlüsseltextstellen:
Teilaufgabe a:
"Every year, road accidents cause the deaths of more than 1,000 young people between the ages of 17 and 21. A teenage driver is seven times more likely to be involved in a fatal accident than a 40-year-old. Road accidents are the most common cause of death in the 15-24 age group." (ll. 7–13)

Teilaufgabe b:
initiator:
"The Government has decided that something must be done to cut these figures. A new training scheme has now started, ..." (ll. 14/15)

target group:
"The scheme is called Pass Plus, and will teach extra skills to young drivers who have already passed their test." (ll. 16/17)

aim:
"The Government has decided that something must be done to cut these figures. A new training scheme has now started, with the aim of helping young drivers to use the roads more safely." (ll. 14–16)

method:
"The course will cost £90 for six one-hour lessons." (l. 18/19)
"The scheme is called Pass Plus, and will teach extra skills to young drivers who have already passed their test." (ll. 16/17)
"There will be no test, but Pass Plus training will have important advantages." (ll. 21/22)

2003-3

"It could be difficult to change this kind of over-confidence with extra train-
ing. Another problem is that as Pass Plus is <u>voluntary</u>, ... " (ll. 32/33)

instructions:
"They will get <u>training in driving at night</u>, on motorways, <u>in towns and coun-
try and in bad weather.</u> " (ll. 17/18)
"<u>Special attention</u> will be paid to <u>the way those taking the course behave to-
wards other road users, and the way they deal with dangerous situations.</u> "
(ll. 20/21)

fees:
The course will cost <u>£90 for six one-hour lessons.</u> " (l. 18/19)

advantages:
"Some insurance companies will <u>make insurance cheaper for people who
have done the course.</u> " (ll. 22/23)

drawbacks/problems:
"<u>Not</u> everyone is <u>certain that the new scheme will help to cut road deaths
among young people.</u> Research has shown that <u>young people usually have
good driving skills.</u> The problem is that <u>they do not use them.</u> " (ll. 26–28)
"It <u>could be difficult to change this kind of over-confidence</u> with extra train-
ing. Another problem is that as Pass Plus is voluntary, <u>the most aggressive
and dangerous new drivers may not take it.</u> " (ll. 32–34)

Darstellungsform / Planung des Notierens:
Als Darstellungsform wird Ihnen das Anfertigen von Notizen vorgeschrieben.
Notizen, die ohne gut erkennbare Strukturierungen angefertigt werden, sind
unübersichtlich und wenig nutzerfreundlich. Bemühen Sie sich daher um sinn-
volles und einheitliches Strukturieren. Teilüberschriften sind dazu sehr ge-
eignet. Arbeiten Sie weiterhin mit Symbolen. Gleichrangige Teilüberschriften/
Aussagen erhalten gleiche Anfangsmarkierungen. Unterordnungen zu einer
Teilüberschrift/Aussage werden mit einer anderen Anfangsmarkierung ver-
sehen.

Teilaufgabe a: Die vorgegebene Hauptüberschrift „Statistics" ist für diesen
Zweck nicht aussagekräftig genug (Welche Statistiken?), d. h. Sie müssen sie
so spezifizieren, dass den nachfolgenden Notizen der richtige Sinn gegeben
wird, z. B. Statistics: Facts and figures on the dangers of being a young
driver. Im Text werden drei gleichrangige statistische Angaben gemacht, die
Sie untereinander auflisten und mit gleichen Anfangsmarkierungen versehen.
Die eigentliche Schwierigkeit besteht in der sprachlichen Form der Notizen.
Formulieren Sie am Anfang Ihres Stichpunktes zunächst den Gegenstand
(z. B. Zahl an tödlichen Verkehrsunfällen pro Jahr bei 17- bis 21-Jährigen:),

den Sie mit einem Doppelpunkt abgrenzen. Dann erst erwähnen Sie den Fakt (1,000). Verfahren Sie mit den beiden anderen Angaben ebenso.

Teilaufgabe b: Auch hier ist es notwendig, die vorgegebene Hauptüberschrift „Pass Plus" zu konkretisieren (Was ist „Pass Plus"?), um den Leser eine inhaltliche Orientierung zu ermöglichen. Formulieren Sie möglichst knapp, worum es bei den nachfolgenden Notizen geht, z. B. Pass Plus – a British training scheme for young drivers. Die Textaussagen hierzu sind nicht alle durchgängig gleichrangig, sodass ein geeignetes Strukturieren notwendig ist. Die Teilüberschriften erhalten identische Anfangsmarkierungen. Auflistungen zu den jeweiligen Teilüberschriften rücken Sie ein und verwenden für diese eine andere Anfangsmarkierung. Bei Kursinhalt ist ein weiteres Untergliedern sinnvoll nach Ausbildung im Fahren und Schwerpunkte.

Statistics: Facts and figures on the dangers of being a young driver
- Number of fatal road accidents a year among 17- to 21-year-olds: more than 1,000
- Likelihood of teenagers being involved in a fatal accident: seven times more likely than a 40-year-old
- Rating of fatal road accidents among deaths of 15- to 24-year-olds: most common cause of death in this age group

Pass Plus – a British training scheme for young drivers
- initiator: British Government
- target group: young drivers who have taken their driving test
- aim: help young drivers to use the roads more safely
- method
  - a course of six one-hour lessons
  - teaching extra skills to young drivers
  - no test
  - course on voluntary basis
- instructions
  - training in driving
    - at night
    - on motorways
    - in towns
    - in country
    - in bad weather
  - focus on
    - participant's behaviour towards other road users
    - participant's way of dealing with dangerous situations
- fees: £90 for six one-hour lessons

- advantages course participants may have: some insurance companies will offer them lower insurance costs
- drawbacks/problems:
  - uncertainty whether the new scheme will help to cut road deaths among young people
  - young drivers usually have good driving skills, but do not use them
  - course might not change the over-confidence of some drivers
  - course might not appeal to very aggressive and dangerous new drivers

2. **Hinweise:** *Sie sollen sich vorstellen, dass Sie für eine Schülerzeitung an einer britischen Schule arbeiten. Ihre Aufgabe ist, einen einseitigen Prospekt für „Pass Plus" zu entwerfen. Sie sollen ein überzeugendes Layout finden und die richtige Sprache, um Ihre Mitschüler für eine Teilnahme an dieser Schulung zu gewinnen. Sie werden weiterhin aufgefordert, einen prägnanten Slogan zu finden und persönlich und provokant zu sein. Symbole und/oder Bilder können verwendet werden.*

Hier wird von Ihnen eine interessante Art der Informationsverarbeitung erwartet, die in besonderem Maße Ansprüche an Ihre Kreativität stellt. Die Auswahl der Informationen unterliegt natürlich bestimmten Zwecken: das Interesse Ihrer Mitschüler wecken und sie zu einer Teilnahme animieren, aber auch das sachliche Informieren über einen solchen Kurs. Nutzen Sie dazu die in Teilaufgabe 1 b verarbeiteten Informationen und wählen Sie Mitteilenswertes aus. Beachten Sie dabei, den sachlich informierenden Sprachstil der Teilaufgabe 1 b nun in eine saloppe, ungezwungene Ausdrucksweise umzuwandeln. Suchen Sie nach einem geeigneten herausfordernden Slogan, dessen Hauptgedanken Sie wie einen roten Faden in Ihren Prospekttexten umsetzen. Zum Schluss verweisen Sie noch auf zwei Dinge: Möglichkeiten der Kontaktaufnahme und Initiator. (Eine Anschrift findet sich in der Aufgabe 2 des B-Teils; Telefonnummer bzw. E-Mail Anschrift werden leider nicht ausgewiesen.) In der Beispiellösung wurde ein momentan aktueller Werbespruch (Geiz ist geil!) in abgewandelter Form genutzt. Zum Wecken des Interesses wird ein lustiges Clipart verwendet mit einer Situation, die jedem Autofahrer wahrscheinlich einmal passiert (In einer Prüfungssituation können Sie nur auf selbst angefertigte Skizzen etc. zurückgreifen). Die darum angeordneten Sprechtexte verfolgen zwei Ziele: den Leser möglichst persönlich ansprechen und zum Leitgedanken (Geiz/Sparen) und zum Slogan (Neues Schulungssystem für geizige Fahranfänger) überzuleiten. Die nachfolgenden Texte haben als Ansatz immer wieder den Spargedanken, informieren dann aber sachlich über Wissenswertes.

Schlüsseltextstellen: siehe Teilaufgabe 1 b

Nutzung der Ergebnisse aus Teilaufgabe 1 b:

Pass Plus – a British training scheme for young drivers
- initiator: British Government
- target group: young drivers who have taken their driving test
- aim: help young drivers to use the roads more safely
- method
  - a course of six one-hour lessons
  - teaching extra skills to young drivers
  - no test
  - course on voluntary basis
- instructions
  - training in driving
    - at night
    - on motorways
    - in towns
    - in country
    - in bad weather
  - focus on
    - participant's behaviour towards other road users
    - participant's way of dealing with dangerous situations
- fees: £ 90 for six one-hour lessons
- advantages course participants may have: some insurance companies will offer them lower insurance costs
- drawbacks/problems:
  - uncertainty whether the new scheme will help to cut road deaths among young people
  - young drivers usually have good driving skills, but do not use them
  - course might not change the over-confidence of some drivers
  - course might not appeal to very aggressive and dangerous new drivers

Darstellungsform:
Siehe hierzu die ausführlichen Hinweise in Übungsaufgabe 6, Lösungen zur Aufgabe 1. Vieles, was dort erläutert wird, trifft analog auch hier zu.

Vom Layout her ist der Prospekt im Lösungsbeispiel andeutungsweise zwei-geteilt. Der obere Bereich dient als Einstieg/Hinführung. Es wird ein Clipart verwendet, um das Leserinteresse zu wecken. Im unteren Bereich geht es dann ganz konkret um „Pass Plus". Symbole aus der Verkehrswelt (Stopp-, Gebots-schild) dienen der Unterstützung der Botschaft. Da der Prospekt insgesamt schon sehr lebhaft wirkt, wurde auf weitere Bilder und Symbole verzichtet.

"You've just taken your driving test? Congratulations!"

"High repair costs? You need to cut your spending?"

"The worst thing which has happened to you so far is a flat tyre? One point for you!"

"How about cutting your insurance costs? – Good idea! – Then don't pass by **PASS PLUS**!"

PASS PLUS – The new training scheme for stingy young drivers

It's hip to grab the bonus insurance companies reward Pass-Plus-certified young drivers with!

For those rare and lucky ones who need not save, we teach you plenty of extra skills, naturally!

Join this form of stinginess to help save your life and other people's!

Stop to Save
and learn
- how to use the roads more safely
- how to behave towards other road users
- how to deal with dangerous situations

Save
and improve your skills in driving
- at night
- on motorways
- in towns
- in country
- in bad weather

Frequently offered courses!

Fees: £90 a course (six one-hour lessons)

No test!

Some insurance companies offer Pass-Plus-certified young drivers incredible cuts in insurance costs!

For more information contact your local branch:
Pass Plus – Young Drivers' Scheme, 7a Belfield Drive, Cardiff Cf2 IUY
An initiative by the British Government

B Creative writing

1. *Hinweis: Versetzen Sie sich in folgende Situation: Sie haben nach einem Discobesuch den letzten Bus verpasst. Ein Freund/Eine Freundin bietet Ihnen an, Sie nach Hause zu bringen, obwohl er/sie zu viel getrunken hat. Aufgabe ist es, aus dieser Situation heraus ein Gespräch zwischen Ihnen und einem Freund/einer Freundin zu verfassen, in welchem Sie über das Dilemma „trinken und fahren" streiten. Geben Sie Ihrem Freund/Ihrer Freundin einen Namen. Nach ein paar kurzen Worten zur Situation (Bus verpasst – damit verbundenes Problem) kommen Sie zügig zum Thema. Versuchen Sie, inhaltlich vielseitig heranzugehen, z.B. Selbstüberschätzung in betrunkenem Zustand, Gefährdung, Polizeikontrolle/Führerscheinentzug, Unfallbeispiel, beleidigtes Reagieren etc. Am Ende Ihres Gespräches sollten Sie zu einer vertretbaren Lösung gelangen. Stilistisch ist eine ungezwungene, jugendgemäße Umgangssprache anzustreben. Beachten Sie beim Notieren, dass die unterschiedlichen Sprecherrollen auch als solche zu erkennen sind.*

Me: Oh no! I don't believe it! The last bus has gone. I must have missed it by a minute!

Daniel: Calm down! No need to worry. Any of my mates will give you a lift.

Me: Yeah, I know, but they won't be leaving for another hour or two.

Daniel: Where's the problem?

Me: I have to be home by one and I'd better be on time tonight.

Daniel: Well, come on then. I'll take you home.

Me: Thanks, Daniel. That's really nice of you. But you've had some drinks, haven't you?

Daniel: A couple of beers. So what? I'm not drunk and I'm perfectly able to drive.

Me: Daniel, you aren't sober. It's far too risky.

Daniel: It's only a short drive and I know my limits. My reflexes are still fine.

Me: Sure. That's what everyone thinks when they're sozzled.

Daniel: Either you need to be home by one or not! Let's go!

Me: No, forget it. Don't risk your driving licence. You know how often there are police spot-checks on a night like this. It's not worth it.

Daniel: Do what you like. I've had enough.

Me: Daniel, don't go off in a huff. It's better this way, believe me. Don't you remember that awful accident Mike had? He's still not OK yet.

Daniel: Maybe you're right.

Me: I'll call a taxi.

Daniel: Well, if you say so.

2. **Hinweis:** *Da Ihnen die Idee von „Pass Plus" zusagt, entscheiden Sie sich, eine Bewerbung für einen solchen Kurs abzuschicken, lautet die Aufgabenstellung. Ihren Brief sollen Sie an die vorgegebene Adresse schicken. Aufgabe ist es somit, sich zu bewerben. Allerdings hat diese Situation wenig zu tun mit einer klassischen Bewerbung für eine Lehr- oder Arbeitsstelle, und der Brief muss inhaltlich entsprechend variiert werden. Günstig scheint es, den Wunsch um Teilnahme mit einer Reihe von Anfragen zum Kurs zu verbinden. Das bedeutet von der Form her, dass Sie eine Mischform zwischen Bewerbungsschreiben und Geschäftsbrief zum Einholen von Informationen anstreben sollten. Beachten Sie die äußeren Merkmale eines Geschäftsbriefes und den typischen Stil.*

Zur Einleitung bietet sich ein Bezug auf den Prospekt aus Aufgabe 2, Teil A an. Dann formulieren Sie Ihren Wunsch um Teilnahme. Begründen Sie Ihren Wunsch mit kürzlich erworbenem Führerschein, Ihren Vorstellungen zum Kursergebnis und z. B. in Aussicht gestellte Senkung der Versicherungsgebühren. Gehen Sie nun zum Erkundigen über. Typische Anfragen beziehen sich z. B. auf Kursbeginn/-zeiten/-ort, benötigte Materialien etc. Bei diesem speziellen Lehrgang ergibt sich z. B. auch die Frage nach dem Fahrzeug, auf dem ausgebildet wird. Schließen Sie Ihre Zeilen mit einem Dank ab und ggf. der Nennung von Anlagen (hier: Kopie des Führerscheins).

Nordhäuser Str. 9
99089 Erfurt
Germany
18 September 2003

Pass Plus – Young Drivers' Scheme
7a Belfield Drive
Cardiff
CF2 IUY
Wales
UK

Dear Sir or Madam

I recently read your advertisement in our school's magazine, and I would like to take part in the young drivers' course you are offering.

I am 18 years old and have just passed my driving test. I feel that the extra skills you teach young drivers would be a good way to improve my driving skills by learning how to use the roads more safely and dealing with dangerous situations. In addition, I have been notified by my insurance company that being Pass-Plus-certified would cut my insurance costs considerably.

Therefore, I am very interested in enrolling for your next young drivers' course.

Could you please supply me with the dates and times of your next course? I would also like to know if I need to bring any materials with me, e.g. the Highway Code.

Finally, could you tell me whether you give the driving lessons in your own vehicles or if I need to bring my own car.

I would be very grateful if you could consider me for your next course.

Please find enclosed a photocopy of my driving licence.

I look forward to hearing from you.

Yours faithfully
Thomas Müller
Thomas Müller

**Besondere Leistungsfeststellung Thüringen 10. Klasse Englisch
2003 – Aufgabe 2**

Slamming with Dirk Nowitzki

* born in Würzburg, Germany
* earns $1.3 million a year
* one of Bavaria's best youth tennis players
* cousin dragged him to basketball practice one day, "just for fun"

Move over Detlef, here comes Dirk. The 20-year-old prodigal hoopster[1] is only the second German to ever make it to the NBA[2]. Across the Atlantic, in central Germany, is the birthplace of basketball's next superstar. Towering seven feet into the air, 20-year-old Dirk Nowitzki grips the ball like a marble[3]. This humble[4] overgrown "Wunderkind", as he has been dubbed by the American media, has graduated from the multi-use gyms of his hometown of Würzburg and stepped up to the "show" – the NBA.

The soft-spoken giant's menacing size and skill have made him the second German next to Detlef Schrempf to run with the biggest of the big boys.

In contrast to his previous life as a minor league basketballer in Germany, Dirk is now living in the land of cowboy hats, thick accents and T-bone steaks; Dallas, Texas, that is. On the night before his first official game with the Dallas Mavericks, Dirk's voice is sprinkled with excitement. "The first weeks at training camp have been brutal. The play here is a lot more physical than back home, but I'm pumped[5] for tomorrow's game," he says.

The first two exhibition games with the Mavericks were good outings for Nowitzki, and Mav[6] coach Don Nelson has a lot of confidence in the youngster. "Dirk is a major piece added to our puzzle," commented Nelson, "We have our small forward[7] and now we are dreaming."

Don Nelson isn't the only one dreaming – how about Dirk? 20 years old, he left his homeland to play in the world's best basketball league. Don't you feel a little overwhelmed with all the pressure, Dirk?

"I stay pretty relaxed," Dirk laughs. "The two games I have played were better than I thought they would be, so we'll just have to wait and see what happens."

Dirk was scouted by the NBA after a tournament for the best college basketballers in the U.S. and the world.

2003-13

35 Outside of basketball, Dirk doesn't have much of a life. "Rookies always have to train extra and they don't get a day off. I don't really have time for much of anything else," explains Nowitzki. But, the $1.3 million a year should probably compensate for his lack of a social life, shouldn't it?

Au contraire[8], says Nowitzki in an interview, "I'm not doing it for the money at 40 all, I just want to succeed as an athlete." Attaboy[9], Dirk.

By Eric St. Gemme (From: Oskar's No. 17, Summer 1999)

Annotations:

1	prodigal hoopster	(slang) outstanding basketball player
2	NBA	National Basketball Association
3	marble	a small ball of glass
4	humble	having no great opinion of one's own importance
5	pumped	highly motivated
6	Mav	short for: Mavericks
7	forward	an attacking player in a team game
8	au contraire	(French) on the contrary
9	Attaboy	(slang) *dt.: Weiter so!*

A Working on the text (25 BE)

Solve the tasks, using your own words as far as appropriate.

1. Read the text about Dirk Nowitzki carefully and present the most important facts about him in a suitable, well-structured way (e.g. mind map, table, ...).
   Use the following categories: facts about Dirk, his early sports activities, Dirk's NBA career and his life in the USA.

2. Scan the text for Dirk's personal statements and use them to give a brief description of his character.

B Creative writing (25 BE)

Choose one of the following tasks. Write a text of at least 200 words.

1. *You are a member of the school basketball team which has been invited to take part in a summer training camp in Dallas. Your team wants to watch Dirk and the Mavericks practising.*
   Write a letter to their coach Don Nelson. Introduce your team, present your tour plan and ask for permission to come. Give good reasons.

2. Money, social life, career?
   What are your dreams and expectations of your future life?

Lösungsvorschläge

A Working on the text

1. *Hinweise: Nach sorgfältigem Lesen des Textes sind die wichtigsten Fakten über Dirk in geeigneter und logischer Weise darzustellen (z. B. in einem Mind Map, einer Tabelle etc.). Folgende Aspekte sind zu berücksichtigen: Fakten über Dirk, seine frühen Sportaktivitäten, Dirks Karriere in der NBA und sein Leben in den USA. Nach dem ersten überfliegenden Lesen des Textes wird bereits deutlich, dass eine unglaubliche Faktenfülle zu verarbeiten ist. Gehen Sie deswegen beim detaillierten Lesen sehr gezielt vor und markieren Sie farblich sortiert alle wichtigen Aussagen zu den vier Aspekten. Spätestens jetzt dürfte deutlich werden, dass aufgrund der Faktenfülle ein Aufgliedern der Aufgabe in zwei große Bereiche sinnvoll ist. Überlegen Sie, welcher Schnitt angebracht sein könnte. Es bietet sich eine inhaltliche Prämisse an. Zum einen die Kurzbiografie Dirks, in der Sie Fakten, frühe Sportaktivitäten und Leben in den USA erfassen (nachfolgend Teilaufgabe a). Zum anderen seine Karriere in der NBA. Stellen Sie diese gesondert dar (nachfolgend Teilaufgabe b). Die Schwierigkeit bei beiden Teilaufgaben besteht in der sinnvollen Ordnung der Fakten, da diese im Text sehr verstreut und nicht chronologisch geordnet sind.*

Schlüsseltextstellen:
Teilaufgabe a: Dirk Nowitzki – A profile
Childhood and youth in Germany
– *place of birth:*
   "born in <u>Würzburg, Germany</u> one of <u>Bavaria</u>'s best youth tennis players ..." (ll. 1, 3)
– *role of sports (sports he did and success):*
   "<u>one of Bavaria's best youth tennis players</u>, cousin dragged him to <u>basketball practice one day</u>, '<u>just for fun</u>'" (ll. 1, 4, 5)
   "In contrast to his previous life as a <u>minor league basketballer</u> in Germany, Dirk ...) (l. 18)
   "Dirk was <u>scouted by the NBA</u> after a tournament for the best college basketballers in the U.S. and the world." (ll. 33/34)
Personality
– *physical features at the age of 20:*
   "Towering <u>seven feet</u> into the air, 20-year-old Dirk Nowitzki grips the ball like a marble. This humble <u>overgrown</u> 'Wunderkind' ..." (ll. 11–13)
   "The soft-spoken <u>giant's menacing size</u> and skill have made him ..." (l. 16)
– *qualities:*
   "This <u>humble</u> overgrown 'Wunderkind' ..." (l. 13)
   "The <u>soft-spoken</u> giant's menacing size and skill have made him ..." (l. 16)

2003-15

Life in the USA:
- *When he went there:*
  "Don Nelson isn't the only one dreaming – how about Dirk? 20 years old, he left his homeland to play in the world's best basketball league." (ll. 28/29)
- *Reason for his move:*
  "Don Nelson isn't the only one dreaming – how about Dirk? 20 years old, he left his homeland to play in the world's best basketball league." (ll. 28/29)
  "This humble overgrown 'Wunderkind', as he has been dubbed by the American media, has graduated from the multi-use gyms of his hometown of Würzburg and stepped up to the "show" – the NBA." (ll. 13–15)
  "On the night before his first official game with the Dallas Mavericks ... (l. 20/21)
- *Where he lives:*
  "In contrast to his previous life as a minor league basketballer in Germany, Dirk is now living in the land of cowboy hats, thick accents and T-bone steaks; Dallas, Texas, that is." (ll. 18–20)
- *training conditions:*
  "'Rookies always have to train extra and they don't get a day off. I don't really have time for much of anything else,' explains Nowitzki." (ll. 35/36)
  "'The play here is a lot more physical than back home, but I'm pumped for tomorrow's game,' he says." (ll. 23/24)

General situation:
- *income:*
  "... earns $1.3 million a year" (l. 37)
- *private life:*
  "Outside of basketball, Dirk doesn't have much of a life. 'Rookies always have to train extra and they don't get a day off. I don't really have time for much of anything else,' explains Nowitzki. But, the $1.3 million a year should probably compensate for his lack of a social life, shouldn't it?" (ll. 35–38)

Teilaufgabe b: Dirk Nowitzki's NBA career
„In contrast to his previous life as a minor league basketballer in Germany, Dirk is now living ..." (ll. 18/19)
"Dirk was scouted by the NBA after a tournament for the best college basketballers in the U.S. and the world." (ll. 33/34)
"'The first weeks at training camp have been brutal.'" (l. 21/22)
"The first two exhibition games with the Mavericks were good outings for Nowitzki, ..." (ll. 24/25)

"... and Mav coach Don Nelson has a lot of confidence in the youngster. 'Dirk is a major piece added to our puzzle,' commented Nelson, 'We have our small forward and now we are dreaming.'" (ll. 25–27)

"On the night before his first official game with the Dallas Mavericks, Dirk's voice is sprinkled with excitement." (ll. 20/21)

"The 20-year-old prodigal hoopster is only the second German to ever make it to the NBA." (ll. 6–8)

"... has graduated from the multi-use gyms of his hometown of Würzburg and stepped up to the "show" – the NBA." (ll. 14/15)

Darstellungsform:

Teilaufgabe a: Dirk Nowitzki – A profile

Die Faktenfülle und deren Aufgliederung in drei große Aspekte spricht für das Mind Map. Beachten Sie beim Erarbeiten das Bezeichnen der Zweige und Unterzweige. Einen großen Zweig widmen Sie Dirks Kindheit und Jugend in Deutschland. Diesen unterteilen Sie in Geburtsort und Rolle des Sports, wobei letztes noch einmal aufsplittbar ist in Sportarten und Erfolge. Mit Persönlichkeit kann der zweite große Zweig beschriftet werden. Sie unterteilen in Körpermerkmale und Eigenschaften. Leben in den USA, der dritte große Zweig, gliedert sich in: wann er dorthin ging, Gründe seines Weggangs, Wohnort, Trainingsbedingungen und Situation allgemein.

Teilaufgabe b: Dirk Nowitzki's NBA career

Dirks Karriere vollzieht sich in Schritten von der Entdeckung seines Talents bis his zum ersten offiziellen Spiel mit dem Mavericks. Demzufolge ist als Darstellungsform ein Flussdiagramm denkbar, in welchem Sie die einzelnen Schritte der Reihenfolge nach aufführen. Bemühen Sie sich um chronologisches Ordnen. Da nur wenige Zeitangaben im Text gemacht werden, wenden Sie Logik in der Abfolge an: Entdeckung – Trainingscamp – Vorstellungsspiele – Nelsons Kommentar nach den Vorstellungsspielen – erstes offizielles Spiel mit den Mavericks und damit gleichbedeutend Aufstieg in die NBA.

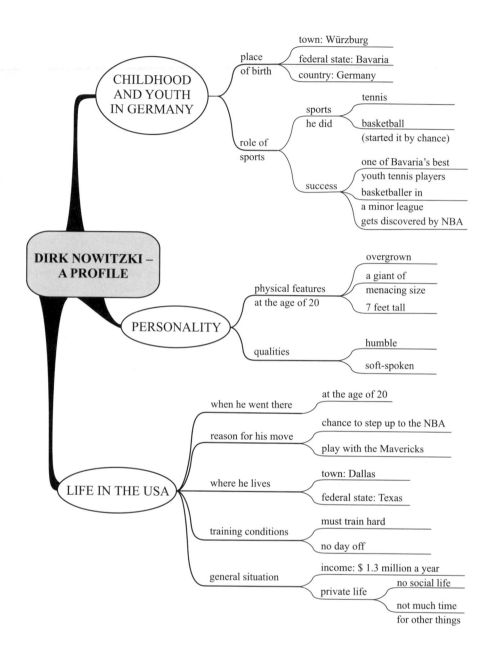

Dirk Nowitzki's NBA career
From a multi-use German gym to the "show" in next to no time

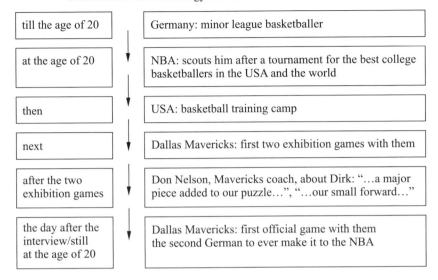

2. *Hinweise:* Suchen Sie den Text gezielt nach Dirks persönlichen Äußerungen ab und nutzen Sie diese für eine Kurzcharakterisierung. Markieren Sie Dirks persönliche Äußerungen und vermerken Sie am Rand, welche Charaktereigenschaften darin zum Ausdruck kommen. In Teilaufgabe 1 a haben Sie bereits zwei im Text direkt genannte Charaktereigenschaften notiert: bescheiden und freundlich. Diese treffen auch bei den Äußerungen zu. Die Kurzcharakterisierung sollte in zusammenhängender Textform erfolgen. Versuchen Sie wenn möglich Ihre Urteile zu begründen.

Schlüsseltextstellen:
qualities: frank, highly motivated, ambitious
"On the night before his first official game with the Dallas Mavericks, Dirk's voice is sprinkled with excitement. 'The first weeks at training camp have been brutal. The play here is a lot more physical than back home, but I'm pumped for tomorrow's game,' he says." (ll. 20–23)
"Au contraire, says Nowitzki in an interview, 'I'm not doing it for the money at all, I just want to succeed as an athlete.'" (ll. 39/40)
qualities: well-balanced, modest
"'I stay pretty relaxed,' Dirk laughs. 'The two games I have played were better than I thought they would be, so we'll just have to wait and see what happens.'" (ll. 31/32)

qualities: hard-working, realistic

"'Rookies <u>always have to train extra</u> and they don't get a day off. I don't really have time for much of anything else,' explains Nowitzki." (ll. 35/36)

Dirk is described as a humble and soft-spoken individual by the author, and this characterization seems to be proved by Dirk's personal statements. Moreover, Dirk appears to be a frank, realistic and well-balanced personality. His humility, frankness and calmness become especially clear when he comments on his exhibition games. When asked about his first official game the following day, he does not display the over-confidence you often find with VIPs. Finally, Dirk seems to be very ambitious and highly-motivated to work hard for his success. It is not the money, but his personal achievements which appear to be the driving force.

B Creative writing

1. ***Hinweis:*** *Sie sollen sich in folgende Situation versetzen: Sie sind Mitglied einer Schulbasketballmannschaft, die zu einem Trainingslager in Dallas eingeladen worden ist. Ihre Mannschaft würde gern Dirk und die Mavericks beim Training sehen. Aus dieser Situation heraus sollen Sie an Don Nelson, den Trainer der Mavericks, schreiben, ihre Mannschaft vorstellen, ihren Aufenthaltsplan darstellen und um Erlaubnis bitten, zu einem Training kommen zu dürfen, sowie Ihr Anliegen gut begründen.*

   Da Ihnen Don Nelson nicht persönlich bekannt sein dürfte, Sie bisher sicherlich keinen Kontakt mit ihm gepflegt haben und Sie sich mit einem Anliegen an ihn wenden wollen, gebietet es die Höflichkeit, dies weitestgehend in Form eines (gemäßigten) Geschäftsbriefes („semi-formal letter") zu tun. Beachten Sie daher die äußeren Merkmale eines solchen Briefes. Leider wird Ihnen in der Aufgabenstellung keine Anschrift zur Verfügung gestellt, sodass Sie diese nur teilweise vermerken können.

   Nachdem Sie sich knapp vorgestellt und Ihr Anliegen (Trainingsbesuch) genannt haben, geben Sie kurze Hintergrunderläuterungen (Ihr Trainingsaufenthalt in Dallas) und begründen Ihren Wunsch. Was Ihren Aufenthalt in Dallas betrifft, sind hier nur wesentliche Informationen sinnvoll (Aufenthaltsdaten und ggf. Termine, die für einen Trainingsbesuch bei den Mavericks nicht in Frage kommen.) Auch Informationen zu Ihrer Gruppe sollten begrenzt sein, z. B. auf Gruppenstärke, Geschlecht, Alter und Begleitpersonen. Das eine oder andere Detail zur Mannschaft lässt sich beim Begründen des Wunsches gut einordnen.

Wöllnitzer Str. 40
07749 Jena
Germany
6 June 2003

The Dallas Mavericks
Mr Don Nelson
Dallas
Texas
USA

Dear Mr Nelson

I am a member of the basketball team at the GutsMuths grammar school in Jena, Germany and I am writing to you on behalf of our team. We would very much like to ask you for permission to come and see the Dallas Mavericks and Dirk Nowitzki train.

Our team will be taking part in a summer training camp in Dallas in July this summer and therefore we were wondering whether it would be possible for you to comply with our wish.

Naturally, being minor league basketballers ourselves, we are very interested in watching the Dallas Mavericks train. It would be the highlight of our training camp in Dallas because your Mavericks players are our great models and we are Dirk Nowitzki fans. Moreover, to see a training session of yours live would be a valuable experience for us.

We will be staying in Dallas from 4–18 July, 2003 and apart from Saturday, 12 and Sunday, 13 July when we will be on outings, any date would suit us. We will be a group of nine boys aged 16 to 18 plus our coach and the local counsellor.

We would be very grateful if you could comply with our request and suggest a date at your convenience.

Thank you for your time, and I look forward to hearing from you.

Yours sincerely

Daniel Bötticher

Daniel Bötticher

2. **Hinweis:** *In dieser Aufgabe geht es um das Darstellen Ihrer Träume und Erwartungen für die Zukunft. Durch die rhetorische Eingangsfrage „Geld, gesellschaftliches Leben, berufliche Laufbahn?" wird Ihrem Text eine Richtung vorgeschlagen, die Sie jedoch nicht zwingend einschlagen müssen. Theoretisch können Sie über jede Art Erwartungen und Träume schreiben. Im Lösungsbeispiel wird jedoch die berufliche Laufbahn aufgegriffen.*

Auch wenn nicht explizit gefordert, gliedern Sie Ihren Text in Einleitung, Hauptteil und Schluss. Für die Einleitung kann z. B. der Wunsch nach dem Blick in die Zukunft genutzt werden. Im Hauptteil stellen Sie dar, was Sie bewegt. Da Sie über Hoffnungen, Wünsche und Träume schreiben, sind Sie sehr stark an die Verwendung des Futurs und des Konditional gebunden. Achten Sie darauf, „will + infinitive" für alle Vorhersagen zu nutzen und „would/ could/should/might + infinitive" anzuwenden, wenn Vorgestelltes formuliert wird. Im Schlussteil bringen Sie Ihre Erwartungen und Wünsche noch einmal kurz auf den Punkt und versuchen, den Kreis zur Einleitung zu schließen.

What will the future bring?

"If only I knew what the future had in store", is a wish most people have. I also wish I knew if my dreams will come true one day. But as there is no way of knowing, let's wait and see. In the following I will write about my dreams and expectations for my life, especially as regards my career.

Being a tenth form pupil at a grammar school, a job and career still seem a long way off to me. Yet, for some time I have been fascinated by the idea of studying to become an interior designer. An experience on our last holiday in Egypt probably set me thinking and dreaming of this career. And the idea grew when one day my art teacher said that I was not without talent as regards drawing and that I had a flair for colours. I suppose such abilities might come in useful in that sort of job. My great dream is to design the interior of functional and prestigious buildings one day, e. g. hotels, guest houses and villas. That would be great. I would not decorate and furnish them in the non-descript, impersonal style that suits all tastes and occasions, but try to give them character and atmosphere.

Anyway, in order to become a popular designer you have to be excellent and plan your career step by step. Next academic year I am specializing in art to get a little closer to my goal. Naturally, I sometimes wonder whether I have taken the right decision and whether my talents will suffice. Let's hope so. Moreover, a lot will depend on my A-level result, because interior design courses are highly in demand. I will need very good grades in most of my subjects to have a chance of a place at university. And that means that I will have to work hard to keep up to the standards. Later on, a course of studies at a foreign university would be great, e. g. in the Middle East, where I could study oriental interior design. Of course, it would be nice to earn good money one day. But I suppose the most important thing is to find fulfilment in your job and to be very good at it. Hopefully, my dreams are not too high-flying and unrealistic and I can live up to my expectations.

In conclusion, I do have dreams and it would be nice if they came true one day. In any case I am willing to work hard for my goals because you are responsible for your own future.

Notizen

Leerseiten verbilligen in diesem Fall die Herstellung des Buches!

Besondere Leistungsfeststellung Thüringen 10. Klasse Englisch
2004 – Aufgabe 1

Branded like Beckham

He has model good looks, a pop-star wife, £15 million worth of sponsorship
deals, and a new contract at the world's biggest football club. David Beckham is
a global marketing phenomenon whose contribution on the field has been
eclipsed by his value off it. The money he has made from his famous right foot is
5 nothing compared to the millions of pounds he has generated in sales for the
football clubs and companies with which he is connected.
At Real Madrid, the 28-year-old England captain is neither the most skilled nor
the most popular in a team full of superstar players. That honour goes to Roberto
Carlos and the local wunderkind Raul.
10 Real Madrid knew that in buying Beckham they had acquired the almost priceless cachet of a popularity that spans continents as easily as it does age, gender
and sexuality. Men want to look like him. Women want to be with him, and
wives see him as an ideal clean-living husband who adores his sons: Brooklyn, 4,
and Romeo, 1. The fashion-conscious copy his clothes and ever-changing hair-
15 styles. At the same time Beckham embraces his status as a gay icon and has been
named the typical "metrosexual": a heterosexual man who enjoys fashion and
other things traditionally associated with women. He is also likely to break into
the American market – less as a footballer than as the male half of one of the
world's most photogenic celebrity couples. The other half is his 29-year-old wife,
20 Victoria, once "Posh Spice" of the Spice Girls. "Posh and Becks" are the most
written-about celebrities in the UK. Their house in England is commonly referred
to as "Beckingham Palace".
While at Manchester United, Beckham was paid £70,000 a week, and the club
paid him a further £20,000 to use his image on promotional materials. But the
25 club did not gain from his personal deals. These include a £3 m contract to promote Adidas; £3 m to endorse children's clothing for Marks and Spencer[1]; £1 m
to appear in Vodafone cellphone adverts; and more than £5 m for promoting,
among other things, chocolates and beauty products in Japan. Beckham's commercial opportunities inspired Real Madrid to negotiate a contract saying that he
30 must give them 50 % of every personal sponsorship deal while at the club.
Real Madrid had its first taste of the pulling power of its new signing[2] when it
went on a tour of the Far East. In China, Beckham's image could be seen on
posters, buses, billboards, TV commercials.

2004-1

Whether or not David Beckham becomes one of Real's key players on the field
35 remains to be seen. Overnight, however, he has become the club's biggest salesman, with worldwide popularity.

From: The Observer, in Spotlight, October 2003

Annotations:

1 Marks and Spencer   British supermarket chain
2 a signing   here: a player under contract

A   Working on the text   (25 BE)

Do the tasks, using your own words as far as possible.

1. Scan the text for information on David Beckham's personal life and his sports career. Present your findings in a clearly structured way (e. g. table, mind map, …).

2. *Imagine you are taking part in an international youth project dealing with celebrities of our time. Your group has the task of portraying David Beckham. Your friend has already written the parts about Beckham's personal life and football career.*
   You are asked to add a short text (circa 100 words) about his business involvement focusing on his time with Manchester United and Real Madrid. Include the visual information on page 3.

B   Creative writing   (25 BE)

Choose one of the following tasks. Write a text of at least 200 words.

1. *"The story of Posh and Becks"*
   Invent a modern fairy tale on the Beckhams using your own imagination and creativity.

   You may start like this:
   Once upon a time there was a small blond boy from England who …

   A possible ending might be:
   … and they lived happily ever after.

2. *Carpe diem – Seize the day*
   Write about ideas for your future life, including values that are important for you.

On the ball: David Beckham was the star of Manchester United's team

Good business: Real will sell a huge quantity of David Beckham's no. 23 shirt

'Zzxllip jjipg klllvvv vcx fjiiikllm David Beckham!'

Cartoon from: Read On, August 2003, Photographs from: Spotlight 10/03

Lösungsvorschläge

A Working on the text

1. *Hinweise: Aufgabe ist es, Informationen zu Beckhams privatem Leben und zu seiner sportlichen Laufbahn in logischer Art und Weise darzustellen. Lesen Sie den Text zunächst überfliegend, um sich einen Gesamtüberblick zum Inhalt des Textes zu verschaffen. Achten Sie dabei darauf, ob die gesuchten Informationen konzentriert in bestimmten Textabschnitten zu finden sind oder ob sie im gesamten Text verstreut sind. Bei zweiten, detaillierten Lesen markieren Sie alle Aussagen. Sie werden dabei feststellen, dass die gesuchten Informationen oft in ganz anderen Zusammenhängen und mitunter nur beiläufig erwähnt werden. Das macht die Informationserfassung schwierig. Lesen Sie ggf. noch ein drittes Mal, um auch wirklich alles Wichtige zu finden. Nun lesen Sie Ihre Textmarkierungen sehr sorgfältig. Sortieren Sie und finden Sie geeignete Gruppierungen/Teilüberschriften, z. B. persönliche Daten, Familie, Club, Zukunft im Fußball, Aussehen, Beliebtheit sowie Marktwert und Einkommen.*

Schlüsseltextstellen:
Persönliche Daten:
"At Real Madrid, the <u>28-year-old</u> England captain is ..." (l. 7)

Club:
"He has model good looks, a pop-star wife, £15 million worth of sponsorship deals, and <u>a new contract at the world's biggest football club</u>." (ll. 1/2)
"At <u>Real Madrid</u>, the 28-year-old England <u>captain</u> is <u>neither the most skilled nor the most popular in a team</u> full of superstar players. That honour goes to Roberto Carlos and the local wunderkind Raul." (ll. 7–9)
"<u>While at Manchester United</u>, Beckham was paid £70,000 a week ..." (l. 23)

Zukunft im Fußball:
"<u>Whether or not David Beckham becomes one of Real's key players on the field</u> remains to be seen." (ll. 34/35)

Familie:
"He has model good looks, <u>a pop-star wife</u> ..." (l. 1)
"The other half is his <u>29-year-old wife</u>, <u>Victoria, once "Posh Spice" of the Spice Girls</u>." (ll. 19/20)
"Women want to be with him, and wives see him as an ideal clean-living husband who adores <u>his sons: Brooklyn, 4, and Romeo, 1</u>." (ll. 12–14)

Aussehen:
"He has model <u>good looks</u>, a pop-star wife ..." (l. 1)

"At the same time Beckham embraces his status as a gay icon and has been named the typical "metrosexual": a heterosexual man who enjoys fashion and other things traditionally associated with women." (ll. 15–17)

Beliebtheit:

"Real Madrid knew that in buying Beckham they had acquired the almost priceless cachet of a popularity that spans continents as easily as it does age, gender and sexuality." (ll. 10–12)

"Overnight, however, he has become the club's biggest salesman, with worldwide popularity." (ll. 35/36)

"Men want to look like him. Women want to be with him, and wives see him as an ideal clean-living husband who adores his sons: Brooklyn, 4, and Romeo, 1. The fashion-conscious copy his clothes and ever-changing hairstyles." (ll. 13–15)

"'Posh and Becks' are the most written-about celebrities in the UK. Their house in England is commonly referred to as 'Beckingham Palace'." (ll. 20–22)

Marktwert und Einkommen:

"David Beckham is a global marketing phenomenon whose contribution on the field has been eclipsed by his value off it." (ll. 2–4)

"Real Madrid knew that in buying Beckham they had acquired the almost priceless cachet of a popularity that spans continents as easily as it does age, gender and sexuality." (ll. 10–12)

"Overnight, however, he has become the club's biggest salesman, with worldwide popularity." (ll. 35/36)

"Beckham's commercial opportunities inspired Real Madrid to negotiate a contract saying that he must give them 50 % of every personal sponsorship deal while at the club." (ll. 28–30)

"He has model good looks, a pop-star wife, £15 million worth of sponsorship deals, and a new contract at the world's biggest football club." (ll. 1/2)

"The money he has made from his famous right foot is nothing compared to the millions of pounds he has generated in sales for the football clubs and companies with which he is connected." (ll. 4–6)

"He is also likely to break into the American market – less as a footballer than as the male half of one of the world's most photogenic celebrity couples." (ll. 17–19)

Darstellungsform/Planung des Notierens:

Als Darstellungsformen werden u. a. die Tabelle und das Mind Map genannt. Eine Tabelle ist jedoch für die Darstellung der gewünschten Informationen nicht geeignet, da Sie nicht vergleichen sollen und eine Tabelle in der Regel die Funktion einer vergleichenden Gegenüberstellung hat. Das Mind Map wäre theoretisch eine geeignete Darstellungsform für die Lösung der Aufgabe, da mehrfach Unterordnungen zu Hauptpunkten vorzunehmen sind. Das Problem besteht jedoch in der Fülle der darzustellenden Informationen. Man würde ein Blatt im A2-Format benötigen, um die Forderung nach Übersichtlichkeit erfüllen zu können. Aus diesem Grund kann auch in den Lösungen kein Mind Map abgebildet werden, da die Größenverhältnisse den vorhandenen Raum sprengen. Als sinnvollste Darstellungsform erweist sich hier die strukturierte Übersicht in Steckbriefart. Notwendige Unterordnungen erreicht man durch das Einrücken und/oder Verwenden verschiedener Symbole für die einzelnen Ebenen.

Besondere Aufmerksamkeit widmen Sie der Ordnung und Eingruppierung der Fakten. Die wichtigsten Aussagen des Steckbriefes (persönliche Daten, Club, Familie) setzen Sie an den Anfang. Die anderen Informationen zu Beckhams Erscheinungsbild, Beliebtheit, Marktwert und Einkommen folgen erst im Anschluss. Bemühen Sie sich um treffenden Ausdruck bei der Bezeichnung der einzelnen Haupt- und Unterpunkte.

Profile

– Name:	David Beckham
– Age:	28
– Job:	football player/world famous football star
– Club:	Real Madrid: the world's biggest football club (former club: Manchester United)
• Position in the team:	captain
• Standing in the team:	not the most skilled not the most popular
– Sporting future:	still unclear whether he will become one of Real Madrid's key players
– Marital status:	married
• wife's name:	Victoria
• her age:	29
• her job:	pop star (once member of the famous "Spice Girls")
– Children:	two sons
• names (age):	Brooklyn (4), Romeo (1)

– **Appearance:**	model good looks
• **provoked image:**	gay
• **enjoyed status:**	"metrosexual": a heterosexual man who enjoys fashion and things usually associated with women
– **Popularity:**	worldwide
• **among men:**	want to look like him the fashion-conscious copy his clothes and ever-changing hairstyle
• **among women:**	want to be with him
• **among wives:**	see him as a model husband appreciate his father role
• **as a couple:**	most written-about British celebrities nickname of their house: Beckingham Palace
– **Marketing value and income:**	
• **for Real Madrid:**	a global marketing phenomenon of priceless popularity worldwide club's biggest salesman half of Beckham's personal income in sponsorship deals while at the club
• **for Beckham himself:**	£ 15 million in sponsorship deals (money from sponsorship deals exceeds his club pay by far)
• **future strategies:**	break into the American market as part of one of the world's most photogenic celebrity couples

2. *Hinweise: Die Aufgabe besteht im Verfassen eines kurzen Textes, in welchem Sie Beckhams Geschäftsbeziehungen darstellen sollen. Dabei sollen Sie sich auf seine Zeit bei Manchester United und bei Real Madrid konzentrieren. Zusätzlich sind die Aussagen der drei beigefügten Bilder einzubeziehen. Beim ersten Lesen haben Sie sicherlich bemerkt, dass sich die benötigten Aussagen im vierten bis letzten Abschnitt konzentrieren. Lesen Sie diese sehr aufmerksam und bemühen Sie sich um genaues Textverständnis. Der Hauptgedanke des vierten Abschnitts ist Beckhams verändertes Einkommen beim Club Real Madrid, an welchen er 50% seiner Sponsorengelder abführen muss. In den anderen Abschnitten wird auf Beckhams Verkaufswert/Werbewirksamkeit eingegangen.*

Schlüsseltextstellen:

"While at Manchester United, Beckham was paid £70,000 a week, and the club paid him a further £20,000 to use his image on promotional materials. But the club did not gain from his personal deals. These include a £3 m contract to promote Adidas; £3 m to endorse children's clothing for Marks and Spencer; £1 m to appear in Vodafone cellphone adverts; and more than £5 m for promoting, among other things, chocolates and beauty products in Japan. Beckham's commercial opportunities inspired Real Madrid to negotiate a contract saying that he must give them 50 % of every personal sponsorship deal while at the club." (ll. 23–30)

"Real Madrid had its first taste of the pulling power of its new signing when it went on a tour of the Far East. In China, Beckham's image could be seen on posters, buses, billboards, TV commercials." (ll. 31–33)

"Overnight, however, he has become the club's biggest salesman, with worldwide popularity." (ll. 35/36)

Bildaussagen:

Foto 1: Beckham wirbt während eines Manchester United Spiels für Vodafone.

Foto 2: Beckham präsentiert für seinen Club Real Madrid ein T-Shirt, dessen Verkaufserlös an den Club geht.

Cartoon: Beckhams Bekanntheitsgrad scheint auch fremde Planeten einzuschließen.

Darstellungsform:

Verfassen Sie einen zusammenhängenden Text, dem Sie eine Überschrift voranstellen. Gliedern Sie Ihre Aussagen in Abschnitte. Im nachfolgenden Lösungsbeispiel wurden auch eine Einleitung und ein Schluss beigefügt, was laut Aufgabenstellung jedoch nicht erwartet wird. Stilistisch runden sie allerdings Ihren Text ab.

Beckham's business involvement

(Being a top football star has always been a very lucrative job. Now employing them seems to be an extra source of income for their clubs as well.)
While playing for Manchester United, Beckham was paid £70,000 a week. Manchester United did not benefit from Beckham's private sponsorship deals. On the contrary, his club even gave him an extra £20,000 to use his image on promotional materials. As a result, he probably had an extra income of more than ten million pounds while the club ended up with nothing.
With Real Madrid, Beckham's financial situation has changed considerably. Beckham has to give half of the money from sponsorship deals to his club. When he is used in advertising now, Beckham's club earns, too. The second

photo shows Beckham advertising himself. This time, however, Real Madrid is the winner. Moreover, the club deliberately profits from Beckham's world-wide popularity (maybe even his cosmos-wide popularity as the cartoon seems to suggest) and uses his image as an extra source of income.
(Is this the price sports stars will have to pay in future?)

B Creative writing

1. *Hinweis: Versetzen Sie sich in folgende Situation: Sie sollen ein modernes Märchen erfinden zum Thema „Die Geschichte von Posh und Becks". Die für ein Märchen typische Einleitung und Schluss werden Ihnen vorgeschlagen.*
   Diese Schreibaufgabe fordert Ihnen ein großes Maß an Vorstellungskraft und Ideenreichtum ab.
   Inhaltlich ist vieles denkbar, vom Ehekonflikt über Untreue in der Partner-schaft bis hin zu Problemen in der Kindererziehung. Ein anderes sehr aktu-elles Thema wäre z. B. die Kehrseite des Berühmtseins.
   Als märchenhafte Elemente können z. B. Fabelwesen wie Zwerge, Hexen, Elfen oder Feen in die Geschichte einbezogen werden. Direkte Rede, einfa-cher Wortschatz und Satzbau sind typische stilistische Elemente.

   The story of Posh and Becks
   Once upon a time, there was a famous English couple called Posh and Becks, whose popularity even reached up to the stars in the sky.
   One day, Posh said to her husband, "Becks, wherever we go we're followed by the Paparazzi. They never leave us alone. I've had enough!" Becks noticed the desperation in his wife's voice. "My dear Posh," he replied, "try to calm down. Tomorrow when the sun shines, everything will be all right again. Don't forget that it is the Paparazzi who make us rich."
   The following morning, Posh was her cheerful self again. "I'm going out shopping," she said happily and left the house.
   A few minutes later, however, the door flew open and Posh rushed back in. Speechless, she threw a tabloid on the table and pointed at it. "POSH AN UNCARING MOTHER – CELEBRITY HITS HER KIDS!" Below the title, a half-page photograph showed Posh in a position where it looked as if she were going to smack their son Brooklyn. "Oh dear, what a shame! But there's nothing we can do about it, darling. That's the freedom of the press!" Becks waited for his wife's reply. Posh moved her lips, but could not get a single word out. The more she tried, the worse it seemed. She had lost her voice. "Oh Posh, you've had a shock. Let's see a specialist. He'll help you."
   But that was easier said than done. The couple went from from one specialist to the next. Not a single one, however, was able to cure her. Terrible months went by. Day after day, Brooklyn and little Romeo asked, "Why won't

Mummy talk to us? Why can't we have chips and ketchup or some ice cream?" Finally, Becks was at his wit's end and plucked up all his courage. "Posh," he said, "let's put Brooklyn and Romeo in a home. We've spent all our money on the doctors, and we've hardly got a penny to our name. Tomorrow we won't even have the money to buy some bread. The press is no longer interested in us. The sponsors are shunning us. We're finished!"

Bitter tears ran down their faces when they stood in front of the children's home, holdings their sons by the hand. "Oh, how I wish we could turn back time and start all over again. We'd never use our popularity to earn our living again. We'd try to live a humble life away from any media bustle."

Suddenly, a fairy appeared. "I'm feeling sorry for you. You've had a terrible time, and you've learnt your lesson. I'll grant you a wish. But choose wisely. You won't get a second chance."

Becks thought hard, but then he knew what he wished for more than anything in the world. "I wish my wife could talk again, so that we could live an ordinary life." "Your wish will come true. But don't you dare sell your popularity ever again, or anyone else's!" the fairy replied, and disappeared in a puff of smoke.

At the very moment, Posh, Becks and their sons found themselves back home again and Posh cried out, "Oh look, the table is laid for dinner!"

Becks and Posh never forgot the fairy's warning and they lived happily ever after.

2. ***Hinweis:*** *In dieser Schreibaufgabe geht es um das Darstellen Ihrer Vorstellungen für die Zukunft. Durch das geflügelte Wort „Carpe diem – Nutze den Tag" wird Ihrem Text eine Richtung vorgeschlagen: Wie wollen Sie Ihre Chancen nutzen? Was wollen Sie aus sich machen? Natürlich bietet sich die berufliche Laufbahn an, die im Lösungsbeispiel auch aufgegriffen wird. Darüber hinaus sollen Sie Ihnen wichtige Werte einbeziehen, z. B. die Bedeutung des Berufes für Sie, die Wichtigkeit, die Geld, Sicherheit, Familie, Partner, Kinder etc. für Sie haben.*

Auch wenn nicht explizit gefordert, gliedern Sie Ihren Text in Einleitung, Hauptteil und Schluss. Für die Einleitung kann z. B. die Aussage „Carpe diem" kurz erklärt werden. Im Hauptteil stellen Sie dar, welche Vorstellungen Sie für die Zukunft haben. Gehen Sie dabei auch auf Werte ein, die für Sie wichtig sind. Da Sie über Hoffnungen, Wünsche und Träume schreiben, sind Sie sehr stark an die Verwendung des Futurs und des Konditional gebunden. Achten Sie darauf „will + infinitive" für alle Vorhersagen zu nutzen und „would/could/should/might + infinitive" anzuwenden, wenn Vorgestelltes formuliert wird. Im Schlussteil bringen Sie Ihre Erwartungen und Vorstellungen noch einmal kurz auf den Punkt und versuchen, den Kreis zur Einleitung zu schließen.

Carpe diem – Seize the day

"Carpe diem", an old saying which goes back to the Roman poet Horace, calls for us to use our opportunities while we can. In my text, I will write about my ideas of what I want my future life to be like, especially as regards my career. I will also discuss values which are important to me.

Being in year 10 at a grammar school, a job and career still seem a long way off to me. Yet, for some time I have been fascinated by the idea of studying to become a biologist. Biology is fun: I like reading and watching scientific programmes about rare animals or plants and species which are in danger of becoming extinct. My great dream is to specialise as an entomologist one day. Entomology is the science of insects. I am fascinated by these little creatures and their incredible varieties. Did you know that insects can be used for solving certain environmental problems? I believe that I could find great fulfilment in the entomological-environmental research field because doing something for our environment by using natural resources would be fantastic. Anyway, I know that working as an entomologist may also mean working abroad in hotter climates. This might not be easy if your partner does not accept it. You need someone understanding at your side or even someone who shares your interests. I do hope that I will find the right partner one day because I would like to have a real family with two or three children. Success in your job is great, but having a family is equally important to me.

In order to become a biologist you have to be excellent and plan your career step by step. Next year I am specialicing in biology to come a little closer to my goal. Naturally, I sometimes wonder whether my talents will suffice. Let's hope so. Moreover, a lot will depend on my A-level results, because biology courses are in great demand. I will need very good grades in most of my subjects to have a chance of a place at university. That means that I will have to work hard to keep up to the required level. Later on, a degree course in entomology at a foreign university would be great, e. g. in Africa or the Middle East. Of course, it would be very helpful and comforting to earn a good salary one day, but I think that finding fulfilment in your job and being very good at it are the more important values.

In conclusion, I am willing to "seize the day" because I am responsible for my own future. Besides success and fulfilment in my job, having a family is equally important to me. Naturally, it would be comforting to earn a good salary one day.

Besondere Leistungsfeststellung Thüringen 10. Klasse Englisch
2004   Aufgabe 3

Shark numbers 'at point of no return'

The ocean's most fearsome predator has become common prey: shark populations have fallen to less than a quarter of their former size in the north-west Atlantic. Some species are approaching the point of no return, and the team that reports the gloomy statistics today warns that current plans for marine reserves will not be
5 enough to stop the decline caused by overfishing. Existing protections for other large marine predators, such as sea turtles and tuna, should be extended to sharks.
Sharks are vulnerable to overfishing because they take many years to mature and have relatively few young per breeding cycle. But they have been increasingly exploited in recent years, both as a "by-catch" and as targets, either for food such
10 as shark fin soup, or as ingredients in health and beauty products.
Researchers at Dalhousie University, Canada, estimate that all the species they studied have declined by more than half in 15 years. The most striking example was hammerhead sharks, down by 89 % since 1988. "The hammerheads concentrate in exactly the same places where the fleets fish for tuna and swordfish,
15 so they are hit because they are at the wrong place at the wrong time," said Professor Ransom Myers, co-author of the report. The sharks routinely feed on the herring and squid commonly used for bait by the long-line[1] fishermen, making catching sharks a routine part of fishing for the other species.
Thresher sharks[2] have declined by 80 per cent. Great white sharks, the predator
20 in the film *Jaws*[3], have dropped by 79 per cent. Tiger sharks have declined by 65 per cent and blue sharks by 60 per cent. "This is a worldwide phenomenon," said Professor Myers. "There are only a few areas in the world where we have enough data, but wherever we do, they show the same thing – the shark is in serious decline."
25 Sharks could be protected by changing commercial fishing patterns. Some of the sharks migrate along set paths at specific times of the year. Prohibiting fishing during those periods could reduce the by-catch of sharks. Also, establishing refuges where all fishing was forbidden would give sharks, along with other fish, a safe haven where they could feed and reproduce safely. The USA has forbidden
30 the harvesting of shark fins for shark fin soup, a favourite in Asia, but long-line fleets from Spain and Japan continue to harvest.
Sharks are at the top of the food chain in the ocean. Experts know from many examples that once you start eliminating the predators at the top it has a ripple effect[4] throughout the food web.

Adapted from The Daily Telegraph, 17. 1. 2003

Annotations:

1	long-line	a single line with thousands of hooks which can be up to 30 miles long
2	thresher shark	Drescherhai
3	Jaws	American title of the film "Der weiße Hai"
4	to have a ripple effect (figurative)	to have far-reaching consequences

A Working on the text

(25 BE)

Do the tasks, using your own words as far as possible.

1. Illustrate the development of the different shark populations in the form of a bar chart.

2. List the reasons that have led to the present situation.

3. According to the text, which measures can be taken to save the sharks? Write a short text.

B Creative writing

(25 BE)

Choose one of the following tasks. Write a text of at least 200 words.

1. Look at the title of the text. Is mankind at the point of no return, too? Discuss this question from your point of view. You may choose issues like environment, health, crime or poverty.

2. You and your friends have heard of plans to build another super-market on a nice site in your neighbourhood where teenagers usually meet.
   Write a letter to your local authorities in which you protest against these plans and ask for their support.

Lösungsvorschläge

A Working on the text

1. *Hinweise: Illustrieren Sie die Entwicklung der verschiedenen Haifischpopulationen in Form eines Säulendiagramms. Lesen Sie zunächst den Text überfliegend, um sich einen Gesamtüberblick zum Inhalt zu verschaffen. Achten Sie dabei bereits auf die entsprechenden Textabschnitte. Die benötigten Aussagen finden sich z. T. im dritten Abschnitt und sehr konzentriert im vierten Abschnitt. Lesen Sie diese genau und markieren Sie alle Fakten wie Name der jeweiligen Haifischpopulation sowie deren Rückgang. Beachten Sie, dass*

2004-13

im Text lediglich Aussagen zum Rückgang der Haifischpopulationen gemacht werden, Aufgabe jedoch ist, deren Entwicklung zu veranschaulichen. Leider finden sich im Text keine Bezugsgrößen, die die Darstellung der Entwicklung ermöglichen. Vermutlich wird von Ihnen folgende Gegenüberstellung erwartet: Prozentsatz an jetzigem Bestand – Prozentsatz des Rückgangs.

Schlüsseltextstellen:
"Researchers at Dalhousie University, Canada, estimate that all the species they studied have declined by more than half in 15 years. The most striking example was <u>hammerhead sharks, down by 89 %</u> since 1988." (ll. 11/12)
"<u>Thresher sharks</u> have <u>declined by 80 per cent</u>. <u>Great white sharks</u>, the predator in the film Jaws, have <u>dropped by 79 per cent</u>. <u>Tiger sharks</u> have <u>declined by 65 per cent</u> and <u>blue sharks by 60 per cent</u>." (ll. 19–21)

Darstellungsform:
Als Darstellungsform wird Ihnen das Säulendiagramm vorgegeben. Legen Sie die Werteachse am günstigsten in 10-Prozent-Schritten an und beschriften Sie diese mit Prozentsatz. Gestalten Sie die Rubrikachse ausreichend breit, um für die zehn Säulen genügend Platz zu haben. Tragen Sie nacheinander jeweils die Säule für den jetzigen Bestand und die für den Rückgang ein, und zwar für alle fünf Haifischarten. Verwenden Sie unterschiedliche Säulenfarben (jetziger Bestand/Rückgang). In der Legende verdeutlichen Sie, welche Farbe wofür steht. Beschriften Sie die Rubrikachse mit den entsprechenden Haifischarten. (Zusätzlich können an den einzelnen Säulen die Prozentwerte vermerkt werden, falls Ihnen die Wertaussagen nicht eindeutig genug sind.) Abschließend wählen Sie eine geeignete Überschrift. Nutzen Sie dazu die Aufgabenstellung.

Development of different shark populations

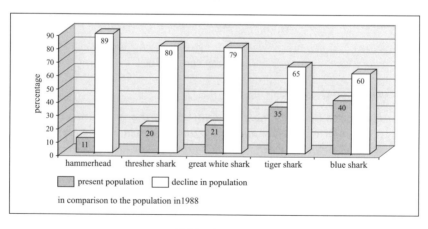

2. **Hinweise:** *Die Aufgabe lautet: Listen Sie die Gründe auf, die zur gegenwärtigen Situation geführt haben. Es ist davon auszugehen, dass hiermit die Gründe gemeint sind, die zum Rückgang der Haifischpopulationen geführt haben. Suchen Sie den Text gezielt nach diesen Informationen ab. Dabei werden Sie feststellen, dass sich diese kompakt in Abschnitt zwei und drei finden. Lesen Sie diese Abschnitte sehr gründlich, vielleicht auch mehrmals, da deren Verständnis schwer sein dürfte. Versuchen Sie zunächst die drei Hauptgründe für den Rückgang zu finden: einerseits Haie als unbeabsichtigter Nebenfang beim Fischen nach anderen Fischarten, Haie als kalkulierte Nebenfangprodukte und drittens Haie als direktes Fangziel. Der Effekt wird zusätzlich noch verstärkt durch biologische Besonderheiten dieser Fischart, z. B. die lange Entwicklungszeit der Haie und deren verhältnismäßig geringe Zahl an Nachkommen.*

Schlüsseltextstellen:
"Sharks are <u>vulnerable to overfishing</u> <u>because they take many years to mature and have relatively few young per breeding cycle</u>. But they have been <u>increasingly exploited</u> in recent years, both <u>as a "by-catch"</u> and <u>as targets</u>, either <u>for food</u> such as shark fin soup, or <u>as ingredients in health and beauty products</u>." (ll. 7–9)
"The <u>hammerheads concentrate in exactly the same places where the fleets fish for tuna and swordfish</u>, so they are <u>hit because they are at the wrong place at the wrong time</u>,' said Professor Ransom Myers, co-author of the report. The <u>sharks routinely feed on the herring and squid commonly used for bait by the long-line fishermen, making catching sharks a routine part of fishing for the other species</u>." (ll. 13–18)

Darstellungsform:
Aufgabe ist es, die Gründe aufzulisten, d. h. sie können eine strukturierte Übersicht anlegen, in welcher Sie untereinander die drei Hauptgründe aufführen. Achten Sie dabei auf notwendige Unterordnungen, wenn Sie weiterführende ursächliche Zusammenhänge notieren. Da es sich nur um drei Hauptgründe handelt, können Sie diese auch nebeneinander anordnen. Bei dieser Anordnung richten Sie die Aufmerksamkeit zunächst gezielt auf die Hauptaussage, die Gründe an sich. Unabhängig von der Form der Übersicht benötigen Sie eine aussagekräftige Überschrift.

Darstellungsform 1: Strukturierte Übersicht

Reasons for the decline in the shark population
– direct target of fishing
- increasing exploitation
  - for food
  - as ingredients in health and beauty products

- **unintentional by-catch**
  - vulnerable to overfishing because
    - take many years to mature
    - relatively few young
    - e. g. hammerhead sharks
      * concentrate where tuna and swordfish live
      * because of this a by-catch of tuna and swordfish catch
- **studied by-catch**
  - catching sharks: a routine part of fishing for other species
    - fishermen take advantage of the sharks' feeding on herring and squid and use them for bait

Darstellungsform 2: Nebenordnende Übersicht

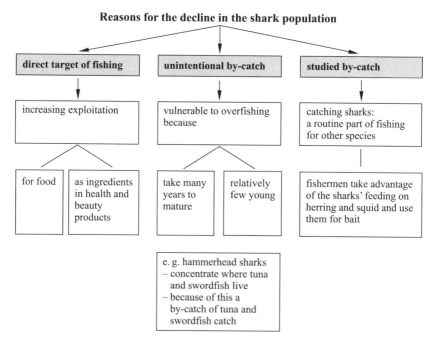

3. *Hinweise: Aufgabe ist es, in einem kurzen Text die Frage zu beantworten, welche Maßnahmen ergriffen werden können, um die Haie zu retten. Die benötigten Aussagen finden sich im fünften Abschnitt. Lesen Sie diesen genau. Für die logische Beantwortung der Frage lesen Sie noch einmal die Lösung zur Aufgabe 2. Hier ging es um die Ursachen für den Rückgang. Ihre Antwort könnte demzufolge als Ansatz haben, wie die in Aufgabe 2 genannten Ursachen abgestellt werden können. Beziehen Sie aber nur Textaussagen ein.*

Schlüsseltextstellen:

"Sharks could be protected by <u>changing commercial fishing patterns</u>. Some of the sharks migrate along set paths at specific times of the year. <u>Prohibiting fishing during those periods could reduce the by-catch</u> of sharks. Also, <u>establishing refuges where all fishing was forbidden would give sharks, along with other fish, a safe haven where they could feed and reproduce safely</u>. <u>The USA has forbidden the harvesting of shark fins for shark fin soup</u>, a favourite in Asia, but long-line fleets from Spain and Japan continue to harvest." (ll. 25–31)

Darstellungsform:

Die Beantwortung der Frage ist in einem zusammenhängenden Text vorzunehmen. Achten Sie auf eine sinnvolle und logische Anordnung Ihrer Aussagen. Nutzen Sie Vokabular des Ordnens („first, second..." oder „one measure, another/a third measure" etc.). Geben Sie Ihrem Text eine Überschrift.

Measures to save the sharks
First, one measure to save the sharks could be to stop the increasing exploitation of sharks for food and other products. Countries could follow the example of the USA, which has forbidden the harvesting of shark fins. Second, changing commercial fishing patterns (e. g. the prohibition of fishing during migration periods) could reduce both the intentional and unintentional by-catch of sharks. A third measure could be the establishment of refuges where all fishing is forbidden and where sharks as well as other fish could feed and reproduce safely. This measure would protect the sharks best because it would tackle all three reasons for their decline.

B Creative writing

1. *Hinweis: Ist die Menschheit am Ende? Gibt es kein Zurück für die Menschheit? Diese Frage sollen Sie von Ihrem Standpunkt aus erörtern. Dabei können Sie sich auf Themen wie z. B. Umwelt, Gesundheit, Kriminalität oder Armut beziehen. Auch andere Themenbereiche wären denkbar. Wählen Sie in jedem Fall ein Thema, über welches Sie gut informiert sind, um stichhaltig argumentieren zu können.*
Gliedern Sie Ihren Text in Einleitung, Hauptteil und Schluss. In der Einleitung führen Sie den Leser zu Ihrem Hauptteil hin und teilen mit, was Sie erörtern wollen. Strukturieren Sie Ihren Hauptteil logisch. Verwenden Sie dazu Vokabular des Ordnens („Let me begin with ... / Now I will discuss ... / Finally, I will write about ...") Geben Sie innerhalb eines Abschnitts mehrere Standpunkte/Argumente, ordnen Sie diese auch („First... / Second... / Furthermore ... / Moreover ... / Finally ..."). Da Ihr Text zu großen Teilen,

Ihre eigene Meinung widerspiegelt, benutzen Sie vielfältige Redewendungen zur Ankündigung Ihrer Anschauungen („In my opinion ..., To my mind ..., I think ..., I believe ... "). Variieren Sie in der Aussagekraft bei strittigen Sachverhalten („I suppose ... / I assume ... ") bzw. bei großer Überzeugtheit („I am convinced ... / I am sure ... "). Im Schlussteil fassen Sie noch einmal kurz zusammen, welche Chancen Sie sehen für die Zukunft.

Is mankind at the point of no return?

You sometimes hear pessimists say that mankind is facing a gloomy future. I do not approve of such ideas because they have a paralysing effect on us. In my text, I will discuss how far mankind may have a future as regards people's health.

Let me begin with the situation today. Live expectancy for both men and women has never been as high. This is a direct result of the very high living standard in developed countries and the progress in medical science. Yet, there are still dangerous diseases like AIDS or cancer. So far, these diseases are not really curable, and more and more people are dying of them. However, in my opinion, it is only a question of time before scientists will have found cures for these diseases as well. I am convinced that we are on the threshold of new medical breakthroughs in the near future.

Now I will discuss what future health problems may arise. First, it is likely that new diseases will develop if we are not careful about what we eat. Here, I am thinking of fast food and genetically engineered food. Unfortunately, fast food is an integral part of our lifestyle today. Scientists are warning of the negative effects the extra doses of vitamins, minerals or hormones may have. To my mind, people do not always pay enough attention to these warnings and believe too easily in the promises made by advertising. Yet, responsibility lies not only in the hands of the individual, but also in the hands of the government. This automatically leads to another side of the problem. As long as industrially engineered foods are cheaper than biologically controlled foods, most people will economise.

Fortunately, as regards genetically engineered food people seem to have more reservations. I believe this general reluctance to consume them is a direct result of the influence of responsible-minded politicians worldwide. This example shows how important political health-consciousness is. Therefore, I am convinced that if people's sense of responsibility towards healthy food increases, mankind will have a future.

Finally, I believe that more health concerns may arise due to the damage we have caused and are still causing to nature. Here, I am thinking of the hole in the ozone layer which has brought about an increase in skin cancer and eye diseases. Allergies may continue to increase over the next few years as an after-effect of decades of polluting our waters and soil. There may even be diseases which nobody has thought of yet. However, I am not that pessimistic. In my opinion, environmental awareness among both politicians and individuals has been growing considerably over the last few years. And that gives me the hope that one day man will manage to live in an acceptable state of harmony with nature.

In conclusion, I do not think that our future will be a gloomy one as regards people's health. I am optimistic. If people's sense of responsibility continues to grow, we will have a chance to overcome unhealthy trends in nutrition and the after-effects of decades of pollution. I do hope that my optimism will be justified in the long run.

2. *Hinweise: Sie sollen sich in folgende Situation versetzen: Sie haben gehört, dass in Ihrer Nachbarschaft ein weiterer Supermarkt geplant ist, und zwar auf einem Gelände, wo sich Jugendliche regelmäßig treffen. Schreiben Sie einen Brief an Ihre Stadt-/Gemeindeverwaltung, in welchem Sie gegen diese Pläne protestieren und um Unterstützung bitten. Diese Aufgabenstellung ist leider sehr formal, da Sie sich in der Regel nicht in der englischen Sprache an eine Behörde in Ihrem Heimatort wenden. Machen Sie jedoch das Beste daraus und konstruieren Sie zweckdienliche Zusammenhänge.*

Ein Brief an eine Behörde fällt unter die Kategorie „formal letter". Beachten Sie daher die stilistischen Merkmale eines solchen Schreibens, welche sich erheblich von privaten Briefen unterscheiden. Bemühen Sie sich um einen logischen Aufbau und klare, aber sehr höfliche Aussagen. Beginnen Sie Ihren Brief mit dem Anliegen, d. h. legen Sie zunächst den Grund Ihres Schreibens dar: gegen den Supermarktplan protestieren und um Unterstützung bitten. Anschließend formulieren Sie Ihre Argumente (z. B. ausreichend vorhandene Einkaufsmöglichkeiten), verweisen auf mögliche Auswirkungen (Vertreiben der Jugendlichen) und machen ggf. Vorschläge. Abschließend bitten Sie noch einmal um Unterstützung. Ordnen Sie alles logisch in einzelne Abschnitte. („First, ..., Second, ..., Furthermore, ..., Finally, ..."). Schließen Sie Ihre Zeilen höflich ab mit einem Bedanken und der Bitte um Rückantwort. Da Ihnen keine Adresse gegeben wird, weichen Sie auf folgende Wendung aus: To whom it may concern.

Heiligenstädter Str. 44
37339 Leinefelde
Germany

To whom it may concern

11 May 2004

Dear Sir or Madam

I am writing to complain about the plan to build another supermarket in our neighbourhood. Moreover, I would very much like to ask you to support our case.

First, I would like to mention reasons for my complaint. In my opinion, the shopping facilities we have already meet the demands of the people. I do not see any necessity for another supermarket in our small town, as there are already three huge shopping centres on the outskirts and several smaller supermarkets in the town centre. Furthermore, the site where the new supermarket is planned, is a popular common where teenagers usually meet.

Second, I would like to write about the effects the destruction of this site may have. Our neighbourhood common is one of the few places where teenagers can still meet in the open. It has an important social function because young people can spend their leisure time there and have fun together. Destroying it would mean to deprive them of this refuge. Moreover, it could push the teenagers away to other places which are less suitable.

Furthermore, I would like to make some suggestions. In my opinion, it would be a good idea to make the existing shopping centres on the outskirts more attractive to customers. This could be done, for example, by setting up a frequent bus service there so that people who have difficulty moving around can get there easily. In addition, more consumer-friendly opening times could be helpful as well.

Finally, I would like to ask you to join in our efforts to stop the plan.

Thank you for your time, and I look forward to hearing from you.

Yours faithfully
Michael Schmidt
Michael Schmidt

| Besondere Leistungsfeststellung Thüringen 10. Klasse Englisch |
| 2005 – Aufgabe 1 |

Around the world in 175 days

80 years ago this month, on 28 September 1924, US Army pilots Eric H. Nelson and Lowell H. Smith landed two airplanes in Seattle, completing the first flight around the world. Done in stages, the journey had taken six months.

Aviation in the 1920s was a dangerous undertaking. By the middle of the decade,
5 for example, one in six airmail pilots in the US had died in a crash. At the same time, the US military wished to find out exactly what possibilities there were in aviation. A flight around the world could answer that question because it presented many challenges of endurance, planning and logistics as well as involving a lot of luck.

10 In parts of the world where aviation was still new, the pilots could not expect to find facilities or fuel. In preparation for a round-the-world flight, 30 extra engines were sent to different parts of the world, and 28 nations along the flight path agreed to provide thousands of litres of fuel and oil. The route itself was set carefully to avoid the problems of seasonal weather, such as monsoons in Asia.

15 Finally, on 6 April 1924, eight army pilots and crewmen left Seattle in four airplanes. Flying westward, they crossed the Pacific at its northern edge, so as to be over land as much as possible. The pilots used the most modern navigational equipment then known, but still had great problems with snow, fog, thunderstorms and sandstorms.

20 On 30 April, one of the planes crash-landed on a mountain in Alaska while flying through thick fog. The pilot and crewman had been walking through the wilderness for 11 days before they were found. The other crews flew on to Japan, south-east Asia, India, the Middle East, Europe, Britain and Ireland. On 3 August, a second plane lost oil and had to land on the water in the windy North
25 Atlantic. Its crew was picked up by a boat five hours later.

After stops in several American cities, Nelson and Smith and their two crewmen triumphantly landed the last two planes in Seattle on 28 September. The 44,360-kilometre journey round the world had taken them 175 days, with 61 stops. Ironically, only nine years later, advances in air travel, plus an automatic pilot
30 and radio direction finder made it possible for the American Wiley Post to fly solo around the world in only eight days.

From: Spotlight, 9/2004 by Mike Pilewski

A Working on the text

(25 BE)

Do the tasks, using your own words as far as possible.

1. Display the chronological order of the events during the six-month journey of the US Army pilots in 1924 in a visual way.

2. Summarise the various problems the pilots were faced with on their tour around the world in a short text.

B Creative writing

(25 BE)

Choose one of the following tasks. Write a text of at least 200 words.

1. Imagine you are one of the pilots. Write a diary entry covering one or more days of this journey.

2. *If anything is to be really done in the world, it must be done by visionaries. (Benjamin Disraeli)*
   Describe how new ideas, discoveries or inventions have made our life easier.

Lösungsvorschläge

A Working on the text

1. *Hinweise: In dieser Aufgabe sollen Sie die Ereignisse im Jahr 1924 während der sechsmonatigen Reise der Piloten der US-Armee in chronologischer Reihenfolge veranschaulichen. Darunter ist zu verstehen, dass Sie möglichst alle wichtigen Daten und dazugehörigen Ereignisse dieser Reise stichpunktartig und zeitlich geordnet notieren. Lesen Sie zunächst den Text sehr genau und kennzeichnen Sie die Passagen des Textes, in denen von der Reise berichtet wird. Lesen Sie nun die betreffenden Textstellen ein zweites Mal genau und markieren Sie alle direkt oder auch indirekt genannten Datumsangaben sowie die dazugehörigen Ereignisse.*

Schlüsseltextstellen:

"80 years ago this month, on 28 September 1924, US Army pilots Eric H. Nelson and Lowell H. Smith landed two airplanes in Seattle, completing the first flight around the world." (ll. 1–3)

"Finally, on 6 April 1924, eight army pilots and crewmen left Seattle in four airplanes." (ll. 15/16)

"On 30 April, one of the planes crash-landed on a mountain in Alaska while flying through thick fog. The pilot and crewman had been walking through the wilderness for 11 days before they were found." (ll. 20–22)

"The other crews flew on to Japan, south-east Asia, India, the Middle East, Europe, Britain and Ireland." (ll. 22 23)

"On 3 August, a second plane lost oil and had to land on the water in the windy North Atlantic. Its crew was picked up by a boat five hours later." (ll. 23–25)

"After stops in several American cities, Nelson and Smith and their two crewmen triumphantly landed the last two planes in Seattle on 28 September. The 44,360-kilometre journey round the world had taken them 175 days, with 61 stops." (ll. 26–28)

Darstellungsform / Planung des Notierens:

Als Darstellungsform bietet sich eine Zeitleiste an, die Sie horizontal oder vertikal anlegen können. Sie ist eine effektive Form der überblicksartigen Darstellung von historischen Ereignissen. Natürlich ist auch eine Tabelle möglich, um die Ereignisse darzustellen. Notieren Sie alle Daten und Ereignisse in zeitlich geordneter Form. Bemühen Sie sich beim Notieren der Ereignisse um Verknappung der Aussagen auf das Wesentliche und verwenden Sie das Präsens. Es kann auch sinnvoll sein, Aussagen mit einer sehr hohen

2005-3

Informationsdichte in zwei Stichpunkte aufzulösen (z. B. "On 30 April, one of the planes crash-landed on a mountain in Alaska while flying through thick fog." – first plane in difficulties due to thick fog, plane crash-lands on a mountain in Alaska). Geben Sie Ihren Notizen eine geeignete Überschrift, damit sich der Leser inhaltlich orientieren kann.

Zeitleiste: About the first flight around the world

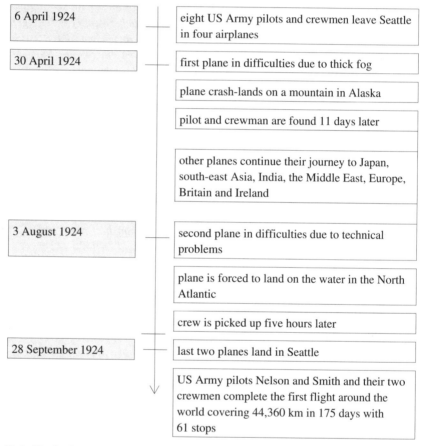

Tabellarische Form: About the first flight around the world

Date	Event
6 April 1924	– eight US Army pilots and crewmen leave Seattle in four airplanes

30 April 1924	– first plane in difficulties due to thick fog
	– plane crash-lands on a mountain in Alaska
	– pilot and crewman are found 11 days later
	– other planes continue their journey to Japan, south-east Asia, India, the Middle East, Europe, Britain and Ireland
3 August 1924	– second plane in difficulties due to technical problems
	– plane is forced to land on the water in the North Atlantic
	– crew is picked up five hours later
28 September 1924	– last two planes land in Seattle
	– US Army pilots Nelson and Smith and their two crewmen complete the first flight around the world covering 44,360 km in 175 days with 61 stops

2. *Hinweise: Hier sollen Sie eine Zusammenfassung zu den einzelnen Problemen der Piloten erarbeiten. Lesen Sie noch einmal den Text und markieren Sie alle relevanten Fakten. Dann ordnen Sie diese nach Aspekten, z. B. allgemeine Probleme, Versorgungsprobleme, Wetter- und technische Probleme.*

Schlüsseltextstellen:

"*Aviation in the 1920s was a dangerous undertaking. By the middle of the decade, for example, one in six airmail pilots in the US had died in a crash. At the same time, the US military wished to find out exactly what possibilities there were in aviation. A flight around the world could answer that question because it presented many challenges of endurance, planning and logistics as well as involving a lot of luck.*" (*ll. 4–9*)

"*In parts of the world where aviation was still new, the pilots could not expect to find facilities or fuel.*" (*ll. 10/11*)

"*The pilots used the most modern navigational equipment then known, but still had great problems with snow, fog, thunderstorms and sandstorms.*" (*ll. 17–19*)

"*On 30 April, one of the planes crash-landed on a mountain in Alaska while flying through thick fog.*" (*ll. 20/21*)

"On 3 August, a second _plane lost oil_ and had to land on the water in the windy North Atlantic. Its crew was picked up by a boat five hours later," (ll. 23–25)

"After stops in several American cities, Nelson and Smith and their two crewmen triumphantly landed the last two planes in Seattle on 28 September. The _44,360-kilometre journey_ _round the world_ had taken them _175 days_, with 61 stops." (ll. 26–28)

Darstellungsform/Planung des Notierens:
Sie sollen den Text kurz zusammenfassen. Schreiben Sie zuerst eine Hinführung zum Thema der Aufgabe. Ihre nachfolgenden Aussagen ordnen Sie dann nach allgemeinen Problemen, Versorgungsproblemen, Wetter- und technischen Problemen. Belegen Sie Ihre Aussagen mit Fakten. Abschließend gehen Sie kurz auf den teilweisen Erfolg ein und runden so Ihren Text ab. Wählen Sie einen nüchternen, knappen und sachlich informierenden Stil.

When four US Army planes started on their flight around the world in 1924, aviation was still a dangerous undertaking. One in six airmail pilots in the US had died in a crash by the middle of the 1920s. Aviation in those days meant many challenges of endurance, planning and logistics because facilities and fuel supplies were not available everywhere. Moreover, extreme weather conditions like fog or sandstorms were still a great problem then involving a lot of luck. However, two of the four planes were out of luck. While one of them crash-landed due to thick fog, the other one was forced to land because of technical problems. Fortunately, nobody was killed. The other two crews were able to triumphantly complete their 44,360-kilometre journey round the world in 175 days.

B Creative writing

1. **Hinweise:** *Stellen Sie sich vor, Sie sind einer der Piloten. Schreiben Sie einen Tagebucheintrag über einen oder mehrere Tage der Reise. Diese Aufgabe steht in engem Zusammenhang zum gelesenen Text, aber es wird ein großer inhaltlicher Spielraum gewährt, da Sie den Piloten und den Zeitraum selbst wählen können. Sie können sich als Figur einen der verunglückten Piloten aussuchen und dessen Flug und Absturz/Notlandung in Ihrem Text darstellen. Wenn Sie sich auf Nelson oder Smith beziehen, bietet Ihnen der Text sehr viele brauchbare Anregungen (z. B. Routenhinweise, Wetterprobleme, Sorge um das vermisste Flugzeug). Ein Tagebucheintrag ist eine sehr persönliche Schilderung von Erlebnissen. Es werden Situationen und Ereignisse wiedergegeben und Gedanken und Gefühle zu dem Erlebten vermerkt. Achten Sie daher beim Ihrem Text auf eine persönlich gefärbte Darstellung. Schreiben*

Sie in einem ungezwungenen Stil. Verwenden Sie umgangssprachliche Formen (z. B. I'm/We're/I've got ...) und umgangssprachliches Vokabular. (in Wörterbüchern gekennzeichnet mit „informal/infml"). Beleben Sie Ihren Text mit Redewendung aus dem mündlichen Sprachgebrauch oder mit emotional gefärbten Wendungen (Thank goodness .../ Fortunately .../Luckily, .../ Oh, God .../ Unfortunately, ...) Erfinden Sie ggf. auch Namen, um die Tagebuchnotizen echter wirken zu lassen.

From Eric H. Nelson's fictional diary

30 April 1924

I'm not so sure whether our plan to cross the Pacific at its northern edge was really such a good idea. We all agreed that we'd only have a chance to succeed if we flew over land as much as possible. Yet, we all knew the risks that might await us in the far north.

Today our worst fears came true. The weather conditions over Alaska were awful. We flew through thick fog for hours and hours praying to God that we wouldn't hit a mountain peak. Smith and his crewman had a narrow escape and it was like a miracle that Tom and I didn't crash on a mountain either. So far three of our four planes have touched down safely at our stop. But the fourth plane hasn't arrived yet. I'm a bit worried because we lost radio contact with them in the late afternoon.

1 May 1924

We still haven't heard anything from the fourth plane. God willing, John and Andrew didn't crash, but were able to make a forced landing out there in the wilderness. We won't give up hope, but we must be prepared for the worst. There are search parties on their way to the area where we last had contact with them. There's no point in our waiting for them any longer. The present weather conditions couldn't be better for crossing the Pacific, so we're continuing our journey to Japan tomorrow.

1 May 1924

Good news today. Thank goodness, our two missing companions have been found! We're so glad John and Andrew are safe. They crash-landed on a mountain in Alaska. Fortunately, they survived the impact and were not seriously injured. But they must have had a terrible time. It's hard to imagine that they had to walk through the cold wilderness for eleven days with only little food and drink. Anyway, tomorrow we're flying on to the Middle East. The weather report says that the sandstorms there have died down and that we can expect a smooth flight over the deserts. If everything turns out alright, we'll have managed more than a third of our 44,000-kilometre journey round the world by tomorrow. Let's hope for the best.

2. **Hinweise:** *Ziel dieser Aufgabe ist das Verfassen eines Textes, in dem Sie darstellen, wie Ideen, Entdeckungen oder Erfindungen unser Leben vereinfacht haben. Bauen Sie Ihren Text logisch auf mit Einleitung, Hauptteil und Schluss. Mit der Einleitung führen Sie den Leser zum Thema hin. Selbstverständlich kann dazu das Zitat aus der Aufgabenstellung als Ausgangsgedanke aufgegriffen werden. Im Hauptteil bemühen Sie sich, Beispiele für Ideen, Entdeckungen oder Erfindungen zu erwähnen und anhand derer ausführlich darzustellen, wie sie das Leben einfacher gemacht haben. Die Beispiele können aus Ihrem persönlichen Umfeld stammen oder sich auch auf das Leben allgemein beziehen (z. B. wichtige Erfindungen der Vergangenheit, Computer, Internet, Haushaltsgeräte, Unterhaltungselektronik, Industrie, Gesundheitswesen). Achten Sie insbesondere darauf, immer wieder zu erläutern, wie sie das Leben vereinfacht haben. Wählen Sie bei der Darstellung von Ideen, Entdeckungen und Erfindungen einen sachlichen Stil. Wenn Sie erläutern, wie unser Leben dadurch vereinfacht wurde, können Sie auch etwas zwangloser formulieren. Darüber hinaus nutzen Sie bewusst sprachliche Mittel der Meinungsäußerung und der logischen Ordnung. Im Schlussteil fassen Sie Ihre Ausführungen kurz zusammen und bringen Wesentliches noch einmal auf den Punkt.*

If anything is to be done in the world, it must be done by visionaries.
(Benjamin Disraeli)

It is hard to imagine what life would be like today without the ideas, discoveries and inventions of the world's greatest thinkers and visionaries. Would we still be hunting for food and cooking our meals over an open fire? Great ideas, discoveries and inventions have changed our lives considerably. In the following, I will discuss how they have made our lives easier.

First, the history of man is a history of constant development. Primitive man probably had the most important vision of all time when he began to use stones as tools about two million years ago. Yet, the visions, discoveries and inventions that have led to the comfortable and easy life we live today are only a few hundred years old. Of the many revolutionary breakthroughs, I suppose the discovery of electricity as a source of power was one of the greatest blessings to mankind. Just imagine Thomas Alva Edison had never had the vision of how to use and generate electricity – would we be living in the digital age? There is hardly any area of industry and business today which does not use electricity to operate machines, computers or computerized machines. These technical devices play such an important role nowadays that production and management would be unthinkable without them. In my opinion, the most important advantage of this development is that people no longer need to do as heavy, tiring work as they did only 50 years ago. Work has become easier for most because automated machines do the heavy labour. As a result, most people live longer and are healthier than ever before. Furthermore, I am convinced that another great advantage of technical development is that automation and computerization have increased productivity enormously, and thus the national income. The average German can afford a good standard of living. People can afford cars, computers, and household and technical equipment, which make daily life much easier and more comfortable.

Now I will discuss how everyday life has become more convenient. As regards housework, I doubt there is a single person who wishes back the old times. Gas and oil heating, fully automated washing-machines, fridges, deep freezers, vacuum cleaners, dish washers, mixers and lots of other devices have made most household chores easier than ever before. Moreover, most devices are so time-saving that there is usually enough time left for hobbies and leisure activities. This is another benefit of technical development: people simply have the time to enjoy the progress in other fields.

Finally, I am convinced that mankind is on the threshold of a new and perhaps dangerous era of progress. Present developments, in the field of genetics for example, show that there is no way of stopping research. Nations like Germany which do not allow research in the field of therapeutic and reproductive genetics at present, will soon fall behind economically. The problem is that the question of cloning is not simply a black and white issue. Just imagine what benefits could be derived from therapeutic cloning one day. It could improve the quality of our life and life expectancy considerably. Let's hope that the responsibly minded visionaries will get their way.

In conclusion, I would say that man's discoveries and inventions have made our lives easier and more comfortable than ever before. It is hard to imagine a life without them. I am convinced that the near future will see another enormous increase in the quality of life. Yet, I hope that the visionaries of our day and age will be able to cope with their responsibility.

Besondere Leistungsfeststellung Thüringen 10. Klasse Englisch
2005 – Aufgabe 2

Optimistic, responsible and political: the face of today's teens

Aren't teenagers supposed to be careless, monosyllabic television addicts, never happier than when sitting in a permanent sulk[1] in their bedrooms?

"Teenagers born after 1985 contrast greatly with Generation X[2]," said Martin Raymond, a director at The Future Laboratory, a London-based trends forecaster,
5 which published a study yesterday. "They are optimistic, socially aware, politically engaged and are concerned about environmental and ethical issues." In this study the behaviour of 2,000 teenagers in the UK and in 15 cities across Europe, including Helsinki, Paris, Tallinn, Berlin, Stockholm and Barcelona was analysed and compared with that of their parents and grandparents. It uncovers a
10 generation of teenagers nicknamed the "Sunshine Teens" who are concerned with a lot of issues earlier generations ignored.

At least 85 per cent of teenagers believe it is necessary to expect brands to be "socially responsible" by emphasising ethical values as opposed to financial value. They may well wear Nike trainers but, at the same time, they are more
15 aware of their relationship to ethical and environmental responsibilities. This is reflected in a rise in anti-brand activism, because teens have become increasingly aware of the Third World exploitation involved in the manufacturing industry. 18-year-old Louise, from Italy, said: "I wouldn't pay money for a T-shirt that had some impressive brand slapped[3] on it that was made in an Indian sweatshop[4]."
20 According to the report the vast majority also feel a strong sense of European identity, with as many as 78 per cent expressing high levels of approval for the EU.

The researchers underlined that, in contrast to the stereotype of moody and angst-ridden teens, optimism and pragmatism were the underlying characteristics
25 found among today's teenagers.

Increased political activism among teenagers is confirmed by rising membership of a growing number of organisations and groups across Europe. "They are definitely more involved in community issues and that is supported by the fact that the number of young people who have joined Greenpeace is unusually high,"
30 Raymond said.

"British teenagers in particular were most preoccupied[5] with health and education, and were completely anti-war. Iraq was an issue that they all felt strongly

2005-10

about," said Mr Raymond. Causes for the increase in political activity among teenagers were partly attributed to events such as 11 September and the Iraqi
35 conflict. However, among British teenagers it was also believed to be linked to the attitudes of their parents as well as recent world events.

Based on: Independent Newspapers Ltd. (March 2004)

Annotations:

1 sulk   period of being silent and bad-tempered
2 Generation X   the people born between 1965 and 1980
3 slapped   *here*: lieblos aufgedruckt
4 sweatshop   Ausbeuterbetrieb
5 preoccupied   to think or worry about sth. very often

A Working on the text (25 BE)

Do the tasks, using your own words as far as possible.

1. Show the positive characteristics and activities of today's teens mentioned in the text in a structured way.

2. Scan the article for at least three aspects of the negative stereotype of teenagers and explain them in a short text.

B Creative writing (25 BE)

Choose one of the following tasks. Write a text of at least 200 words.

1. Describe your picture of today's teens including your personal experiences.

2. Within a European exchange programme you have found some young people interested in joining you in your summer holiday trip.
   Write a letter to them about your group's travel plans, interests and hobbies.

Lösungsvorschläge

A Working on the text

1. *Hinweise:* *Die Aufgabe besteht in der systematischen Darstellung der positiven Eigenschaften und Aktivitäten der heutigen Teenager. Dieses Thema ist sehr allgemein formuliert und verlangt von Ihnen eine tiefgründige Auseinandersetzung. Da in großen Teilen des Textes Aussagen hierzu zu finden sind, müssen Sie besonders sorgfältig beim Lesen und Markieren sein. Lesen Sie den Text zunächst einmal gründlich durch, um den Sinngehalt zu erfassen. Beim zweiten Lesen konzentrieren Sie sich auf das Erkennen von bestimmten inhaltlichen Aspekten: Welche inhaltlichen Aspekte werden beleuchtet? Wozu werden Ihnen Informationen gegeben? Sie werden feststellen, dass sich die Textaussagen im wesentlichen drei Aspekten zuordnen lassen:*
   1. allgemein wertende Aussagen zu den heutigen Teenagern,
   2. Aussagen zum politischen und ethischen Bewusstsein sowie zum Umweltbewusstsein der Jugendlichen heute und
   3. Aussagen zu deren Aktivitäten auf politischer und ethischer Ebene sowie auf Umweltebene.
   Beim Markieren der relevanten Textstellen nutzen Sie ggf. verschiedene Farben für das Kennzeichnen der drei Aspekte oder vermerken stichpunktartig die Zugehörigkeit zu dem jeweiligen Aspekt.

Schlüsseltextstellen:
1. Allgemein wertende Aussagen zu den heutigen Teenagern

"'They are optimistic, socially aware, politically engaged and are concerned about environmental and ethical issues.'" (ll. 5/6)

"In this study the behaviour of 2,000 teenagers in the UK and in 15 cities across Europe, including Helsinki, Paris, Tallinn, Berlin, Stockholm and Barcelona was analysed and compared with that of their parents and grandparents. It uncovers a generation of teenagers nicknamed the 'Sunshine Teens' who are concerned with a lot of issues earlier generations ignored." (ll. 6–11)

"The researchers underlined that, in contrast to the stereotype of moody and angst-ridden teens, optimism and pragmatism were the underlying characteristics found among today's teenagers." (ll. 23–25)

"'British teenagers in particular were most preoccupied with health and education, and were completely anti-war. Iraq was an issue that they all felt strongly about,' said Mr Raymond. Causes for the increase in political activity among teenagers were partly attributed to events such as 11 September and the Iraqi conflict." (ll. 31–35)

2005-13

2. **Aussagen zum politischen und ethischen Bewusstsein sowie zum Umweltbewusstsein der Jugendlichen heute**

"_At least 85 per cent of teenagers believe it is necessary to expect brands to be 'socially responsible' by emphasising ethical values as opposed to financial value_. They may well wear Nike trainers but, at the same time, they are more aware of their relationship to ethical and _environmental responsibilities_. This is reflected in a rise in anti-brand activism, because teens _have become increasingly aware of the Third World exploitation involved in the manufacturing industry_. 18-year-old Louise, from Italy, said: '_I wouldn't pay money for a T-shirt that had some impressive brand slapped on it that was made in an Indian sweatshop_.'" (_ll. 12–19_)

"According to the report the _vast majority_ also _feel a strong sense of European identity_, with as many as _78 per cent expressing high levels of approval for the EU_." (_ll. 20–22_)

"'_British teenagers_ in particular were most preoccupied with health and education, and were _completely anti-war_. Iraq was an issue that they all felt strongly about,' said Mr Raymond. Causes for the increase in political activity among teenagers were partly attributed to events such as 11 September and the Iraqi conflict." (_ll. 31–35_)

3. **Aussagen zu deren Aktivitäten auf politischer und ethischer Ebene sowie auf Umweltebene**

"They may well wear Nike trainers but, at the same time, they are more aware of their relationship to ethical and environmental responsibilities. _This is reflected in a rise in anti-brand activism_, because teens have become increasingly aware of the Third World exploitation involved in the manufacturing industry." (_ll. 14–17_)

"_Increased political activism_ among teenagers is _confirmed by rising membership of a growing number of organisations and groups across Europe_. 'They are _definitely more involved in community issues_ and that is _supported by the fact that the number of young people who have joined Greenpeace is unusually high_,' Raymond said." (_ll. 26–30_)

"'_British teenagers_ in particular were most preoccupied with health and education, and were _completely anti-war_. Iraq was an issue that they all felt strongly about,' said Mr Raymond. Causes for the _increase in political activity among teenagers were partly attributed to events such as 11 September and the Iraqi conflict_." (_ll. 31–35_)

Darstellungsform / Planung des Notierens:

Auch das systematische Darstellen der erfassten Fakten verlangt von Ihnen sorgfältige Überlegungen im Vorfeld. Notizen, die ohne gut erkennbare Strukturierungen (z. B. Teilüberschriften) angefertigt werden, sind unübersichtlich und wenig nutzerfreundlich. Bemühen Sie sich daher um sinnvolles und einheitliches Strukturieren. Teilüberschriften sind dazu sehr geeignet. Formulieren Sie deshalb die bereits gefundenen Aspekte zu Teilüberschriften (z. B. General statements about today's teens, Findings as regards their political, ethical and environmental consciousness, Findings as regards their political, ethical and environmental activities). Arbeiten Sie mit Symbolen. Gleichrangige Teilüberschriften/Aussagen erhalten gleiche Anfangsmarkierungen. Unterordnungen zu einer Teilüberschrift/Aussage werden mit einer anderen Anfangsmarkierung versehen. Setzen Sie Ihren Notizen eine Überschrift voran, um den Leser inhaltlich zu orientieren.

Positive characteristics and activities of today's teens

- **General statements about today's teens**
  * European teenagers
    – optimistic
    – socially aware
    – politically engaged
    – concerned about environmental and ethical issues
    – concerned with a lot of issues earlier generations ignored
    – pragmatic
  * British teenagers in particular
    – preoccupied with health and education
    – completely anti-war

- **Findings as regards their political, ethical and environmental consciousness**
  * expect manufacturers of brand-name articles to be socially responsible
  * ethical values of greater importance to them than financial values
  * more awareness of their ethical and environmental responsibilities
  * increasing awareness of the Third World exploitation in the manufacturing industry
  * a strong sense of European identity
  * 78 % approval of the EU
  * British teenagers in particular completely anti-war

- **Findings as regards their political, ethical and environmental activities**
  * rise in anti-brand activism
  * increase in political activism
  * a rising membership of a growing number of organisations and groups across Europe
  * stronger involvement in community issues
  * unusually high number of young people who have joined Greenpeace

2. *Hinweise: Mindestens drei Aspekte von negativen Stereotypen/Klischeevorstellungen bezüglich Teenager sollen in einem kurzen Text erklärt werden. Überfliegen Sie dazu den Text noch einmal und markieren Sie die geäußerten Klischeevorstellungen. Leider wird in der Aufgabenstellung nur gesagt, dass Sie die Klischeevorstellungen erklären sollen. Zu erklären, was z. B. sorglos, einsilbig, fernsehabhängig, launisch usw. ist, macht aber wenig Sinn. Gemeint sein dürfte sicherlich, diese Klischees zu kommentieren. Gehen Sie also von Folgendem aus: Stellen Sie zunächst die genannten Klischees dar. Dann kommentieren Sie diese. Sie können z. B. darstellen, dass Klischeevorstellungen oft auf zu starker Verallgemeinerung beruhen, dass diese Stereotype sicherlich auf einen Teil der Jugendlichen zutreffen, aber nicht auf die Jugend insgesamt. Als eine weitere Ursache für das hartnäckige Bestehen von Klischees gegenüber Jugendlichen können Sie erwähnen, dass oft die veränderten gesellschaftlichen Bedingungen nicht berücksichtigt werden usw. Nutzen Sie als weiteres Argument auch die im Text erwähnte Studie, die die Klischees widerlegt.*

Schlüsseltextstellen:

"Aren't teenagers supposed to be <u>careless, monosyllabic television addicts, never happier than when sitting in a permanent sulk in their bedrooms</u>?" (ll. 1/2)

"The researchers underlined that, in contrast to the <u>stereotype of moody and angst-ridden</u> teens, optimism and pragmatism were the underlying characteristics found among today's teenagers." (ll. 23–25)

Darstellungsform/Planung des Notierens:

Als Darstellungsform wird Ihnen ein kurzer Text vorgegeben. Versuchen Sie Ihren Ausführungen etwas Struktur zu geben, indem Sie zuerst die Klischees nennen, bevor Sie diese dann kommentieren. Ordnen Sie Ihre Aussagen/Argumente logisch und verwenden Sie entsprechendes Vokabular des Ordnens bzw. Aufzählens (z. B. Moreover, .../Furthermore, ...) Runden Sie Ihre Ausführungen ggf. mit einem abschließenden Satz ab.

The clichés that are mentioned in the text claim that today's teenagers are careless, watch too much TV and are not sociable. Moreover, it is said that the teens of today are introverted, moody and angst-ridden. Naturally, like any other cliché, these stereotypes have developed from experiences people have had, and they contain some truth. The problem is that such negative experiences are often grossly generalized and exaggerated. Of course, there are teenagers to whom these characteristics may apply, but in my opinion, they are not true for all young people. Furthermore, when today's adults were young, life circumstances were different and they seem to forget this when they criticize young people's TV consumption, for example. Our parents or grandparents did not have the opportunities teens have today and this is probably another reason why the differences in lifestyle often result in negative stereotypes. In conclusion, clichés are usually gross generalizations which are seldom true for the great majority of people and the study mentioned in the text supports this.

B Creative writing

1. *Hinweise: Beschreiben Sie Ihr Bild von heutigen Jugendlichen und beziehen Sie eigene Erfahrungen ein, so lautet das Thema dieser Schreibaufgabe. Dabei handelt es sich um eine einsträngige Darstellung Ihrer Anschauungen. Setzen Sie sich zunächst intensiv mit dem Thema auseinander. Man gelangt sehr schnell zu Aussagen, wie: „Die Jugendlichen heute sind ungezwungen, früh selbstständig und unabhängig. Sie akzeptieren Autorität nicht unkritisch, sondern hinterfragen ..." Problematisch ist jedoch, diese Anschauungen zu einem homogenen Text zusammenzufügen. Setzen Sie sich daher einen oder mehrere Schwerpunkte, z. B. Lebensgefühl und Lebensstil, Verhalten anderen gegenüber, Einstellung zu Schule und berufliche Laufbahn, Freizeitverhalten. Dann bearbeiten Sie den/die Schwerpunkte. Im Beispiel wurde der Schwerpunkt Lebensgefühl und Lebensstil gewählt. Der Hauptteil setzt sich aus drei großen Abschnitten zusammen. Im ersten Abschnitt werden Anschauungen zunächst allgemein geäußert. Der zweite Abschnitt zeigt Beispiele und Zusammenhänge auf. Der letzte Abschnitt verweist auf ein Problem und erläutert dieses. Wenn die Stoffsammlung zum Hauptteil abgeschlossen ist, arbeiten Sie an einer geeigneten Einleitung. Diese kann in klassischer Form erfolgen, indem Sie das Thema konkret aufgreifen. (In the following I will describe my picture of today's teens and mention some experiences ...) Ein passendes Zitat als Ausgangspunkt zu wählen, wie es im Beispiel getan wurde, dürfte unter Prüfungsbedingungen sicherlich schwierig sein. Trotzdem soll Ihnen diese Möglichkeit hier aufgezeigt werden. In Schlussteil bringen Sie Ihre wichtigsten Gedanken noch einmal kurz auf den Punkt.*

2005-17

Finden Sie abschließend eine Überschrift zur Orientierung des Lesers. Bemühen Sie sich in Ihren Darlegungen um einen sachlichen Sprachstil. Da Sie immer wieder sehr persönliche Anschauungen äußern, kündigen Sie Ihre Meinung entsprechend an (In my opinion, .../To my mind, ...*/I think/believe/ suppose ...).*

Today's teens and their attitude towards life

"Nowadays, young people love luxury. They have bad manners, despise authority, do not show respect to their elders and natter when they are supposed to be working. They contradict their parents, ... and tyrannize their teachers."

How old do you think this quote is? Some ten or twenty or even fifty years? You couldn't be more wrong! This quotation is about 2400 years old and goes back to the Greek poet and philosopher Socrates. It is hard to imagine that the behaviour of young people has been the subject of criticism for such a long time.

In the following I will describe my view of today's teens and mention some experiences I have had. I will narrow down my thoughts to the attitude of today's teens towards life and discuss this in greater detail.

In my opinion, modern teens' attitude towards life is no worse or better than that of their parents and grandparents – it is just different. The biggest difference is probably that the teenagers of today want to take charge of their own lives at a much earlier age. They like to make their own decisions and do what they think is best when they are still quite young. I believe that one of the positive aspects of this is that today's teens grow up much faster. Moreover, they learn to stand their ground and to take responsibility for their actions in good time. Thus, they are prepared early on for future life.

This increased sense of independence and self-assertion shows in a lot of fields of everyday life, particularly at school and in their free time. School and teachers have lost their importance and influence. The average pupil no longer sees school and teachers uncritically, but questions their authority and work. As a result, pupils have a more casual attitude towards education and instructors. Of course, a lot of pupils usually do their homework and prepare for tests, but they often spend as little time as possible on this. Leisure time, entertainment and fun are equally important to them. I think this is alright because you are only young once and school is not everything. After all, it is everybody's own business to set their goals.

However, a negative aspect of this increased sense of independence and self-assertion is that young people usually do not have the money they need for their lifestyle. Let's take the example of clothes. Being stylish means a lot to most young people, but fashionable clothes are expensive. Quite a number of

my schoolmates are really mad about brand-name clothing and it is not nice that they look down on pupils who cannot afford them. There is a lot of peer pressure and teens start to tyrannize their parents until they give in. The same applies to a lot of other everyday things like going out during the week or partying on the weekends.
So after all, Socrates' two thousand-year-old criticism still seems to be true in a way.
In conclusion, I would say that young people today are no worse or better than generations of teens before them. You are only young once and it is the right of the young to enjoy life however they want.

2. **Hinweise:** *Stellen Sie sich vor, Sie haben während eines europäischen Austauschprogramms Jugendliche kennen gelernt, die gern mit Ihnen in Sommerurlaub fahren möchten. Schreiben Sie einen Brief an diese Jugendlichen über die Reisepläne Ihrer Gruppe, Ihre Interessen und Hobbys. Beachten Sie die äußeren Merkmale eines solchen Schreibens. Inhaltlich vorgegeben wird folgende Situation: eine Gruppenreise, bereits bestehende Pläne für den gemeinsamen Sommerurlaub sowie Interessen und Hobbys dieser Gruppe. Sie können Ihrer Fantasie relativ freien Raum lassen, was Ort und Art des Sommerurlaubs betrifft. Wählen Sie aber in jedem Fall eine Urlaubsart und eine Feriengegend, zu der Sie über ausreichend Sachwissen und über genügend Vokabular verfügen. Städteaufenthalte, Urlaub am Meer oder Campingurlaub bieten sich sicherlich an. Im nachfolgenden Beispiel wird eine Kleingruppe von Freunden gewählt, die mit zwei weiteren Jugendlichen den Sommerurlaub verbringen möchte. Selbstverständlich können Sie auch einen anderen Ausgangspunkt wählen. Verwenden Sie einen sprachlich ungezwungenen Stil und umgangssprachliche Formen, z. B. Kurzformen (I'm/We're/ I've got ...) und wenn möglich umgangssprachliches Vokabular. (Dieses ist in Wörterbüchern in der Regel mit „informal/infml" gekennzeichnet.) Beleben Sie Ihre Zeilen, indem Sie z. B. durch Fragen oder Hinweise auf die Briefpartner eingehen.*

Langensalzaer Str. 10
99089 Erfurt
Germany

10th May

Hi Andrew and Steven,

Thanks a lot for your letter and the photos. How's life? Have you taken all your exams yet? We've nearly finished and so far everything has gone well for most of us.

It's great that you're thinking of joining us on our holiday trip. Then there'll be six of us: you, three friends of mine and me.

Now – more about our plans. As you already know, we want to go hiking on a new trail around Lake Edersee. Have you ever heard of that lake? Probably not. It's a relatively big lake in the north of the Federal State of Hesse. The new trail there is called "Urwaldsteig" – jungle trail in English. But it's not a tropical jungle, of course, it's a primeval forest where we'll be hiking. The trail is about 70 km long and said to be very wild and romantic in unspoilt scenery. Hikers should be fit because the path is a bit difficult in some places. Of course, we won't be hiking all the time. We'll have a stop over every 10 or 12 km and pitch our tents. Will that be alright for you? There'll be enough time for other things every day and the Edersee is just great for all kinds of water sports: sailing, surfing, swimming etc. My friends and I are very keen swimmers. What about you? Then there are sailing and surfing schools along the lake and let's hope that we can try a bit of sailing and surfing there as well. I'm sure that we'll have a lot of fun together.

Anyway, we'll start on 30 July. It's a Saturday and my parents will take us there in their van. It's about a two-hour drive away from here. By the way, there's room for eight people in the van – no need to worry! So how about spending a day or two with me and my family before we leave for the Edersee together? Please let me know what you think. We hope to make the trail in a week and will return the following Saturday. Then someone else's parents will fetch us.

Now let's see what things you need to bring. Can you bring your own tent, air mattresses and sleeping bags? You needn't worry about any other camping equipment as we'll take that. Good hiking shoes and weatherproof clothes are important though, and don't forget your swimming trunks. There are lots of snack booths, little pubs and shops all around the lake, so food and drink will be no problem.

Well, if you've got any more questions about our hiking trip, please let me know. I'll try to answer them immediately.

I'm really looking forward to our holiday together and can hardly wait!

Yours,

Georg

Besondere Leistungsfeststellung Thüringen 10. Klasse Englisch
2006 – Aufgabe 1

The world loves SpongeBob SquarePants

What is square, yellow, and loved by under-10s, students and celebrities? The answer is SpongeBob SquarePants, the biggest yellowish cartoon sensation since The Simpsons.

The cheerful rectangular sponge who lives in a pineapple at the bottom of the ocean is going to achieve world domination when "SpongeBob SquarePants – the Movie" opens in cinemas on Friday. In the US, the tie and trouser-wearing sponge already has a huge celebrity fan base, including Britney Spears, Justin Timberlake, and Bruce Willis. Next week in the UK, the children's network Nickelodeon is showing episodes of the cartoon on its animation channel Nicktoons in the winter holidays, in a so-called "SpongeBobathon"[1].

SpongeBob, who first appeared on American television in 1999, is the creation of Stephen Hillenburg, a former marine scientist – but the cartoon is not scientific at all. The character lives underwater in Bikini Bottom, where he works as a cook at the Krusty Krab Diner and keeps a pet snail called Gary who miaows like a cat. His best friends are a pink starfish called Patrick and a female squirrel[2] called Sandy Cheeks, who wears a helmet so that she can breathe underwater.

In 2004, 9.7 million viewers watched SpongeBob on Nickelodeon channels, including two fifths of all children in the UK and it is now the top-rating show on Nicktoons. The cartoon is very successful and has earned a reported £ 400 million since 2002.

Originally targeted at seven-to-nine year olds, SpongeBob's charm is growing among adults who like the cartoon's strange humour. Howard Litton, Nickelodeon's director of channels, said: "There seems to have been a groundswell[3] over the past 12 months. In some ways it's like The Simpsons when it first launched. Although it's targeted at kids, it has become popular with adults and it's cool in student circles. It has got huge support because of its craziness and its silliness. People enjoy the optimism of SpongeBob."

2006-1

In the US, however, right-wing groups have tried to uncover a darker side to
35 SpongeBob, blaming the cartoon's creators for promoting homosexuality to children. There are rumours that SpongeBob is gay because he holds hands with his friend Patrick. The producers say that there is no hidden message in the cartoon and they insist that it is intended to help teach children about co-operation and unity.

40 Report by Ciar Byrne
Media Correspondent

From: The Independent, Feb. 10, 2005 (adapted and shortened); Photo: © UIP/Cinetext

Annotations:
1 "SpongeBobathon" word formation of SpongeBob and marathon
2 squirrel *dt.:* Eichhörnchen
3 groundswell *dt.:* Welle der Begeisterung

A Working on the text (25 BE)

Cartoons are very popular with people of different ages. For a presentation in class, you have selected SpongeBob SquarePants.

Do the tasks, using your own words as far as possible.

1. Make a written profile of SpongeBob. Categorise the information about this character in a well-structured way.
2. Prove that the statement of the heading is correct. Write a short coherent text about SpongeBob's success.

B Creative writing (25 BE)

Choose one of the following tasks. Write a text of at least 200 words.

1. Introduce one of your favourite films, books or TV series *(except SpongeBob SquarePants)*. Explain why it has impressed you so much.
2. *In today's modern world, people tend to go to extremes or to search for the kick.*
   Describe the cartoon (on page 4) and link it to the free-time interests and activities of your friends and yourself.

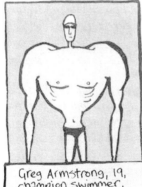

In: Pop Culture, Language Skills in context 1, Max Hueber Verlag 2005, p. 56
© *International Language Teaching Services Pty. Ltd.*

Lösungsvorschläge

A Working on the text

1. **Hinweise:** *Folgende Situation wird der Aufgabe vorangestellt: Zeichentrick-filme sind sehr beliebt bei Menschen unterschiedlichen Alters. Für eine Prä-sentation im Unterricht haben Sie SpongeBob SquarePants ausgewählt. Sie sollen eine Art Steckbrief zu SpongeBob verfassen und die Informationen zu dieser Figur logisch strukturieren und gruppieren. Das heißt, sie sollen alle Aussagen zu SpongeBobs Persönlichkeit, wie z. B. Herkunft, Wohnort, Tätig-keit, Charaktereigenschaften usw. systematisch nach einem Ordnungsprinzip auflisten. Lesen Sie zunächst den Text sehr genau und kennzeichnen Sie die Passagen des Textes, in denen Aussagen zu SpongeBobs Persönlichkeit ge-macht werden. Lesen Sie die betreffenden Textstellen ein zweites Mal und mar-kieren Sie alle direkt oder indirekt genannten Persönlichkeitsmerkmale.*

Schlüsseltextstellen:

"What is square, yellow, *and loved by under-10s, students and celebrities?" (ll. 1–3)*

"The cheerful rectangular sponge *who* lives in a pineapple at the bottom of the ocean *is going to achieve world domination when 'SpongeBob Square-Pants – the Movie' opens in cinemas on Friday. In the US,* the tie and trou-ser-wearing sponge *already has a huge celebrity fan base, including Britney Spears, Justin Timberlake, and Bruce Willis. Next week in the UK, the chil-dren's network* Nickelodeon *is showing* episodes of the cartoon *on its ani-mation channel Nicktoons* in the winter holidays, in a so-called *'Sponge-Bobathon[1]'." (ll. 7–16)*

"SpongeBob, who first appeared on American television in 1999*, is the* creation of Stephen Hillenburg, a former marine scientist *– but the cartoon is not scientific at all. The character* lives underwater in Bikini Bottom*, where* he works as a cook at the Krusty Krab Diner *and keeps* a pet snail called Gary who miaows like a cat*. His* best friends *are* a pink starfish called Patrick *and a* female squirrel[2] called Sandy Cheeks*, who wears a helmet so that she can breathe underwater." (ll. 17–22)*

"People enjoy the optimism of SpongeBob*." (l. 33)*

Darstellungsform / Planung des Notierens:

Als Darstellungsform bietet sich eine strukturierte Auflistung an. Gleicher-maßen ist aber auch die tabellarische Form denkbar. Notieren Sie alle Daten in geordneter Form. Bemühen Sie sich um sinnvolle Kategorisierung: Identity (Person), Background (Herkunft): Creator/Father, Date of first appearance/Date of birth, Place of first appearance/Place of birth, Where he lives, Characteristic features ... Wählen Sie eine geeignete Überschrift.

Profile: SpongeBob

Identity:	– cartoon character
Background	
Creator:	– Stephen Hillenburg, a former marine scientist
Date of first appearance:	– 1999
Place of first appearance:	– American television
Where he lives	
Location:	– underwater – at the bottom of the ocean
Place name:	– Bikini Bottom
Home:	– in a pineapple
Looks	
Body:	– yellow rectangular sponge
Clothes:	– tie – trousers
Traits:	– cheerful – optimistic
Job:	– cook at the Krusty Krab Diner
Miscellaneous	
Pet:	– Gary, a pet snail (miaows like a cat)
Friends:	– Patrick, a pink starfish – Sandy Cheeks, a female squirrel (a helmet helps her to breathe underwater)

2. *Hinweise: Aufgabe hier ist der Nachweis der Behauptung aus der Über-schrift, dass die Welt SpongeBob SquarePants liebt. Dies soll in zusammen-hängender Textform erfolgen. Lesen Sie noch einmal den Text und markie-ren Sie alle Aussagen, die im Zusammenhang mit SpongeBobs Beliebtheit ge-macht werden. Beim Markieren werden Sie bemerken, dass sich die Autorin eigentlich auf Großbritannien beschränkt mit wenigen Bezügen zu den USA. Die erwähnten Nickelodeon Sender haben natürlich sehr viele Stationen weltweit. Aber die Zahl von 9,7 Millionen Zuschauern in 2004 würde auf die Welt bezogen bedeuten, dass SpongeBob ein Flop ist. Diese Zahl scheint auf Großbritannien allein zuzutreffen. Ähnliches gilt für den erwähnten Gewinn von £400 Millionen seit 2002. Darüber hinaus ist Howard Litton Direktor der britischen Nickelodeon Sender. Sie können also keinen wirklichen Nachweis auf die Welt bezogen führen. Grenzen Sie daher Ihren Nachweis auf Großbritannien ein mit einem kurzen Verweis auf die USA.*

Schlüsseltextstellen:

"What is square, yellow, and <u>loved by under-10s, students and celebrities?</u> The answer is SpongeBob SquarePants, the <u>biggest yellowish cartoon sensation since The Simpsons."</u> (ll. 1–6)

"The cheerful rectangular sponge who lives in a pineapple at the bottom of the ocean <u>is going to achieve world domination</u> when 'SpongeBob Square-Pants – the Movie' <u>opens in cinemas on Friday</u>. In the US, the tie and trouser-wearing sponge already has <u>a huge celebrity fan base, including Britney Spears, Justin Timberlake, and Bruce Willis."</u> (ll. 7–14)

"<u>In 2004, 9.7 million viewers watched SpongeBob on Nickelodeon channels, including two fifths of all children in the UK and it is now the top-rating show on Nicktoons. The cartoon is very successful and has earned a reported £ 400 million since 2002."</u> (ll. 23–26)

"Originally targeted at seven-to-nine year olds, <u>SpongeBob's charm is growing among adults who like the cartoon's strange humour.</u> Howard Litton, Nickelodeon's director of channels, said: '<u>There seems to have been a groundswell³ over the past 12 months. In some ways it's like The Simpsons when it first launched. Although it's targeted at kids, it has become popular with adults and it's cool in student circles. It has got huge support because of its craziness and its silliness. People enjoy the optimism of SpongeBob.'</u> " (ll. 27–33)

Darstellungsform/Planung des Notierens:

Als Darstellungsform wird Ihnen ein kurzer Text in zusammenhängender Form vorgegeben. Leider lässt sich der Text nicht wirklich kurz fassen, da zunächst die Einschränkung auf Großbritannien erfolgen sollte. Außerdem lautet die Aufgabe, einen Nachweis zu führen (keine Zusammenfassung), und dieser ist mit Fakten zu belegen.

Erwähnen Sie zunächst, warum Sie Ihren Nachweis auf Großbritannien (und die USA) beschränken. Ihre nachfolgenden Aussagen ordnen Sie dann nach Erfolg in britischen Nickelodeon-Kanälen, Erfolg unter Erwachsenen und Ursachen. Belegen Sie Ihre Aussagen mit Fakten aus dem Text. Abschließend gehen Sie kurz auf die Vermutung des Autors bezüglich des bevorstehenden Kino-Erfolgs weltweit ein. Wählen Sie einen knappen und sachlich informierenden Stil.

The world loves SpongeBob SquarePants

This statement by Ciar Byrne, the author of the text, is probably true. However, her text mainly refers to Great Britain and in parts to the USA. Thus Byrne's text is not really open to an interpretation of the cartoon's worldwide popularity and I cannot prove that this statement is correct.

However, I will try to prove that the British love SpongeBob.

As regards the British Nickelodeon channels, the facts speak for themselves: the British love the yellow sponge and even seem to be crazy about him. In 2004, for example, 9.7 million people (including two fifths of all children) watched SpongeBob. In the winter holidays in 2005, a SpongeBobathon followed. Not only that, in 2005 SpongeBob was the top-rating show on Nickelodeon's animation channel. The cartoon has brought in £400 million since 2002 and seems to be the biggest sensation since The Simpsons.

Although originally aimed at children, the cartoon has also won incredible popularity among adults and in student circles. In the USA, there is even a huge celebrity fan base. The reasons for this SpongeBob mania may be the optimism of the main character and the cartoon's craziness and silliness. In 2005 the movie opened in cinemas and the author of the text put forward the idea that the character of SpongeBob was going to achieve world domination.

B Creative writing

1. *Hinweise: Stellen Sie Ihren Lieblingsfilm, ihr Lieblingsbuch oder ihre Lieblingsfernsehserie vor. Erklären Sie, warum es Sie so beeindruckt hat. Schreiben Sie einen Text von wenigstens 200 Wörtern. Beachten Sie aber, dass es sich dabei lediglich um eine Mindestwortzahl handelt.*

   Diese Schreibaufgabe eröffnet Ihnen einen sehr breiten inhaltlichen Spielraum. Theoretisch denkbar sind alle fiktiven und (populär-) wissenschaftlichen Werke aus Literatur, Film und Fernsehen, die bei Ihnen bleibende Eindrücke hinterlassen haben. Ihre Darstellung darf sich jedoch nicht auf eine Inhaltsangabe beschränken. Wählen Sie in jedem Fall ein Werk, zu dem Sie Ihre Eindrücke ausführlich darstellen können. Etwas Spannendes oder anderweitig tief Beeindruckendes bietet sich an. Auch wenn nicht explizit gefordert, strukturieren Sie Ihren Text in Einleitung, Hauptteil und Schluss. Leiten Sie Ihren Text in interessanter Weise ein, z. B. mit einer rhetorischen Frage, einer Behauptung oder einem Slogan. Im Hauptteil stellen Sie möglichst knapp die Handlung/den Inhalt dar und möglichst nur dann, wenn es zum Verständnis zwingend notwendig ist. Gehen Sie gezielt zur Darstellung Ihrer Eindrücke über und erklären Sie, warum es Sie beeindruckt hat. Mit Ihren Schlussbemerkungen schlagen Sie einen gedanklichen Bogen zur Einleitung.

Dan Brown: The Da Vinci Code

You are crazy about high-energy thrillers. At the same time you like to read about art, history and mythology. You want to be entertained from the first to the last page. Then try *The Da Vinci Code* by Dan Brown. Once you have started it, you will not be able to put it down, I am sure.

The Da Vinci Code, Dan Brown's latest novel, is not simply a detective story or a murder hunt. It is a brilliant mixture of crime, mythology, little known historical facts, an incredible analysis of *The Last Supper* by Da Vinci and shocking interpretations of Catholic legends. The many amazing facts and clever fictional ideas in the novel impressed me deeply and I will probably read it again some day.

The novel begins with a strange murder in the Louvre in Paris. The French Police call in the American professor Robert Langdon who is an expert on ancient symbols. Sophie Neveu, the granddaughter of the murder victim, joins Langdon. Together they try to solve the mysterious secret that died with Sophie's grandfather. A thrilling treasure hunt begins. With keen interest I followed the hero and heroine on their exciting chase from one clue or puzzle to the next. I always hoped that the next clue would finally shed light on the mystery. But the author always leads you to a new mystery which is even more difficult to solve than the one before. In this way Dan Brown grabs your attention brilliantly and I simply could not stop reading.

During their treasure hunt Robert and Sophie have to deal with ancient mythology, a secret society and the history and legends of Christianity. Impressive historical or scientific facts are revealed. Again and again, you marvel: *Incredible! How amazing!* or *No! I can't believe that!* To give a good example, you read about Jesus and his twelve disciples in Da Vinci's painting *The Last Supper*. In the novel, the disciple next to Jesus is seen as a woman – Mary Magdalene. You learn about the role this woman might have played in Jesus' life. But I found it very hard to "swallow" these interpretations. All the time, you are surprised or even shocked at what you are reading. Long-standing Catholic values and ideas are turned upside-down. I constantly asked myself whether it might be true or whether it was pure fiction. Thus, Dan Brown's novel sets you thinking. He permanently forces you to decide all for yourself whether you are just reading some piece of dubious fiction or whether Brown is telling the plain truth. The author challenges you to form your own opinion. And that is never easy, you can believe me.

All in all, I do not think that *The Da Vinci Code* is a really deep novel, and it is probably not very intellectual either. Yet, reading it was good fun and I think that Brown's latest novel is very entertaining and impressive. Now, of course, the movie is being shown in the cinemas. I am going to watch it. Let's see whether the film version can live up to the standards of the novel.

In conclusion, I recommend *The Da Vinci Code* to anyone who likes a really good mixture of suspense, art, history and mythology, amazing facts and dubious fiction. And, if nothing else, the novel challenges you to think and decide for yourself!

2. **Hinweis:** *In unserer modernen Welt zieht es die Menschen hin zum Bezwingen von Extremen oder zur Suche nach dem Kick – so lautet der Leitgedanke zur Aufgabenstellung. Beschreiben Sie den Cartoon und bringen Sie ihn in Verbindung mit den Freizeitinteressen und -aktivitäten Ihrer Freunde und Ihren eigenen.*

Diese Schreibaufgabe stellt hohe Anforderungen an Ihre sprachliche Versiertheit. Sie ist weiterhin sehr komplex aufgrund Ihrer Zweiteiligkeit: Beschreibung des Cartoons und Herstellung von Verbindungen zu Freizeitinteressen Ihrer Freunde und zu Ihren eigenen. Beachten Sie, dass es sich bei der vorgegeben Wortzahl lediglich um eine Mindestwortzahl handelt. Allein für ein aussagekräftiges Beschreiben des Cartoons werden Sie zwischen 150 und 200 Wörter benötigen.

Gliedern Sie Ihren Text in Einleitung, Hauptteil und Schluss. Leiten Sie Ihren Text ein, z. B. mit einer provokanten Aussage oder einer rhetorischen Frage. In Beispiel unten wurde außerdem eine klassische Ankündigung des Schreibgegenstandes vorgenommen aufgrund der Komplexität des Themas.

Den Hauptteil selbst unterteilen Sie in zwei oder drei Komplexe: Beschreibung des Cartoons, Interpretation seiner Aussage und Herstellung der Verbindung zu Freizeitinteressen Ihrer Freunde bzw. Ihren eigenen. Versuchen Sie in Ihre Aussagen auch den Leitgedanken zur Aufgabenstellung einzubeziehen. Im Schlussteil fassen Sie wesentliche Ergebnisse Ihrer Auseinandersetzung kurz und bündig zusammen.

About massive muscles and more

Broad shoulders, muscular upper arms and thighs and six-pack at all costs? In the following I will describe a cartoon about three freaks. I will try to interpret the message the cartoon communicates and link this to the leisure interests and activities of myself and my friends.

Let me begin by describing the cartoon. It consists of three separate illustrations and depicts three freaks, Greg Armstrong, Phil Leggett and Tom Preston, whose keen interest in different activities has had a strong effect on their bodies. Their family names are just like omens which have ironically come true. A caption under each of the three pictures gives additional information about their age and their activities. Being 19, the three boys are still teenagers, yet their bodies are unnaturally developed for their age.

Greg Armstrong, the freak in the left-hand picture, is a champion swimmer and has been swimming since he was eight. Greg's arms seem to be very strong indeed ("Armstrong"). He has developed very broad shoulders and bulging muscles in his upper arms and in the upper part of his body. His overdeveloped upper body is probably the result of very intensive training day after day for years.

The freak in the middle picture, Phil Legget, is all legs. He has got such massive, muscular thighs that his cycling shorts seem to be bursting. No wonder! He started cycling at the age of eleven and has probably trained very hard ever since. Like Greg, he is a champion in his sport. Unfortunately, his upper body has remained childlike.

Tom Preston, the video game freak in the right-hand picture, has been pressing the buttons on gameboys ever since he was a small boy of three and a half. His thumbs have grown to alarming proportions, unfit for everyday life. Yet, he has been very successful and is a champion, too.

Second, I will try to link the cartoon's message to the leisure interests and activities of myself and my friends. The main question the cartoon raises is whether excessive training is worth the consequences it may have on your body (and personality). Of course, I respect Greg's, Phil's and Tom's efforts and admire their success. But look at their body proportions. Do they really appeal to you? As far as I am concerned, they do not! Therefore, I think that each individual should decide for himself what priorities he establishes and whether sporting success is more important to him than any possible consequences connected with it.

None of my friends are sports freaks, although most of us go in for some kind of sport or other activities, of course. My friend Rebecca, for example, is an enthusiastic badminton player and a member of a club. She regularly attends training. But badminton does not dominate her life. I am a water sports fan and usually go swimming once a week. But excessive training of any kind does not really entice me. I have a lot of other interests from surfing the net to watching TV to reading.

However, I know a girl at my school who is absolutely obsessed with aerobics and slimming. She has been attending spinning classes for some time, and she goes four or even five times a week. She says it is the ultimate kick – the burst of adrenaline – during the extreme workout which fascinates her. Last week, however, she had to be taken to hospital because of serious problems with her spine. She will not be able to attend school for the next few weeks. Her example shows that going to extremes can be risky. All in all, I believe that all sports or activities carried to the extreme will cause either health problems or other difficulties sooner or later. I find it hard to understand people who just do it for the kick they get from it.

In conclusion, I respect and admire all sportsmen and women. But excessive training entices neither my friends nor me. We are simply not prepared to go to extremes or to search for the ultimate kick at all costs.

| Besondere Leistungsfeststellung Thüringen 10. Klasse Englisch |
| 2006 – Aufgabe 2 |

Exploring Britain

Oxford

Oxford is a town of culture and history. It is dominated by 36 university colleges, the most famous being Christ Church. The High Street has been referred to as 'One of the world's great streets', and once you wander along it, you will under-
5 stand why.

If you're looking for the nightlife, head across Magdalen Bridge to Cowley Road. Here you will find the student district, which has a number of good pubs and clubs. Enjoy! If you are the more active type of person, go punting along the River Thames from Magdalen Bridge or climb onto Carfax Tower to get a bird's
10 eye view of the High Street. For culturally interested people, the Oxford Play-house offers classical drama, comedy, music and much more and – Christ Church is simply a must.

Due to its proximity[1] to London, Oxford is a popular weekend break. It is strongly recommended that you stay longer.
15 Contact Oxford Tourist Information for more things to do.

Glastonbury

This small market town in the county of Somerset has a colourful ambience and for many, this area is considered to hold deep spiritual energies. Funky cafés, quirky shops, colourful people and unusual events mix together to make Glas-
20 tonbury a great spot to hang out for a while.

Glastonbury Tor, which stands on a hill overlooking the town, is probably the most famous sight here. There are many myths and legends regarding its origins. A local tour will keep you informed. A famous attraction is Glastonbury Abbey, whose ruins are set in 37 acres of parkland. Some people believe King Arthur
25 was buried here alongside with his Queen Guinevere.

Made famous for its awesome summer music festival, there are also many lesser known festivals in Glastonbury. In March the town hosts the annual Majma dance festival, a celebration of the best in Middle Eastern and North African dance and culture with a mixture of dance performances, workshops, seminars
30 and delicious traditional food stalls. Check out www.glastonbury.co.uk for more details.

Cardiff

Cardiff is a delight to visit at any time of the year, whether there's a special event on or not. A real buzz of excitement fills the city of Cardiff when there's a match

35 on at the Millennium Stadium. Picture over 70,000 screaming fans chanting their songs!

In season, a cheap boat ride from behind the Millennium Stadium will take you to the ultra modern Cardiff Bay. On a warm spring day. enjoy a bite to eat at one of the pavement cafes. If the weather's bad then check out the Techniquest[2]
40 science museum at Mermaid Quay for a real 'hands on' experience.

The Museum of Welsh Life is rapidly becoming Wales' most popular heritage attraction. The open air museum stands in the grounds of the magnificent 16th century St. Fagan's Castle in Cardiff.

Enjoy exploring of this vibrant Welsh town, which is at the same time Europe's
45 youngest capital city.

Annotations:

| 1 | proximity | near in distance |
| 2 | Techniquest | word formation of technique and quest |

A Working on the text   (25 BE)

*Your group is planning a trip to Great Britain at the end of class 10.
You come across a travel magazine in which you find descriptions of
different holiday destinations.*

Do the tasks, using your own words as far as possible.

1. List the attractions of the three places and the activities you can do
   there.

2. Say, in not more than two sentences each, what kind of towns Oxford,
   Glastonbury and Cardiff are.

3. Decide which of the three holiday spots you would prefer. Give reasons for your choice. Write a short coherent text.

B Creative writing   (25 BE)

Choose one of the following tasks. Write a text of at least 200 words.

1. Make up a dialogue between a teenager and their parent(s) in which
   they discuss a trip the young person has planned with friends.

2. *Languages can build bridges ...*
   Show that the knowledge of foreign languages helps to connect people
   in various spheres of life. You may include tourism, music, the world
   of work ...

Lösungsvorschläge

A Working on the text

1. **Hinweise:** *Versetzen Sie sich in die vorgegebene Situation: Ihre Gruppe plant eine Fahrt nach Großbritannien am Ende der Klasse 10. Sie finden in einer Reisebroschüre Beschreibungen zu unterschiedlichen Ferienzielen. Aufgabe ist, die Attraktionen der drei vorgestellten Orte aufzulisten sowie Aktivitäten, die Sie dort unternehmen können.*
   Lesen Sie zunächst den Text sehr genau und kennzeichnen Sie alle direkt oder indirekt genannten Attraktionen und möglichen Aktivitäten. Es ist eine hohe Anzahl an Fakten im Text enthalten und die Schwierigkeit dieser ansonsten relativ einfachen Aufgabe liegt in der Erfassung möglichst aller Details.

   Schlüsseltextstellen:
   Oxford
   "It is <u>dominated by 36 university colleges</u>, the <u>most famous being Christ Church</u>. The High Street has been referred to as '<u>One of the world's great streets</u>', and once you wander along it, you will understand why." (ll. 2–5)
   "If you're looking for the <u>nightlife</u>, head across Magdalen Bridge to <u>Cowley Road</u>. Here you will find the <u>student district</u>, which has <u>a number of good pubs and clubs</u>. Enjoy! If you are the more active type of person, <u>go punting along the River Thames from Magdalen Bridge</u> or <u>climb onto Carfax Tower to get a bird's eye view of the High Street</u>. For <u>culturally interested people</u>, the <u>Oxford Playhouse</u> offers <u>classical drama, comedy, music and much more</u> and – <u>Christ Church is simply a must</u>." (ll. 6–12)

   Glastonbury
   "This small market town in the county of Somerset has a <u>colourful ambience</u> and for many, this <u>area is considered to hold deep spiritual energies</u>. <u>Funky cafés, quirky shops, colourful people and unusual events</u> mix together to make Glastonbury a <u>great spot to hang out for a while</u>." (ll.17–20)
   "<u>Glastonbury Tor</u>, which stands <u>on a hill overlooking the town</u>, is <u>probably the most famous sight</u> here. There are many myths and legends regarding its origins. <u>A local tour</u> will keep you informed. A famous attraction is <u>Glastonbury Abbey, whose ruins are set in 37 acres of parkland</u>. <u>Some people believe King Arthur was buried here alongside with his Queen Guinevere</u>." (ll. 21–25)
   "Made famous for its <u>awesome summer music festival</u>, there are also <u>many lesser known festivals</u> in Glastonbury. <u>In March</u> the town hosts the <u>annual Majma dance festival, a celebration of the best in Middle Eastern and North African dance and culture with a mixture of dance performances, workshops, seminars and delicious traditional food stalls</u>." (ll. 26–30)

Cardiff
"Cardiff is a delight to visit at any time of the year, whether there's a special event on or not. A real buzz of excitement fills the city of Cardiff when there's a match on at the Millennium Stadium. Picture over 70,000 screaming fans chanting their songs!" (ll. 33–36)
"In season, a cheap boat ride from behind the Millennium Stadium will take you to the ultra modern Cardiff Bay. On a warm spring day, enjoy a bite to eat at one of the pavement cafes. If the weather's bad then check out the Techniquest² science museum at Mermaid Quay for a real 'hands on' experience." (ll. 37–40)
"The Museum of Welsh Life is rapidly becoming Wales' most popular heritage attraction. The open air museum stands in the grounds of the magnificent 16ᵗʰ century St. Fagan's Castle in Cardiff." (ll. 41–43)

Darstellungsform/Planung des Notierens:
Die tabellarische Form ist sicherlich die effektivste Darstellungsformen für diese Aufgabe. Für drei unterschiedliche Orte sollen zwei verschiedene Aspekte dargestellt werden, also eine klassische Tabelle mit drei Spalten und drei Zeilen plus Kopfzeile. Es sind jedoch sehr viele Fakten zu jedem einzelnen Ort zu verarbeiten, so dass eine zusätzliche Zeilenunterteilung bei jedem Ort sinnvoll ist. Das erhöht die Übersichtlichkeit. Außerdem können Sie so Attraktion und dazugehörige Aktivitäten in einen schlüssigen Zusammenhang bringen.
(Auch die strukturierte Auflistung und das Mind Map sind denkbar, wobei hier die erforderlichen Teilüberschriften bzw. Zweigbezeichnungen die Notizen sehr aufwändig gestalten.)

Place	Attractions	Activities
Oxford	36 university colleges, e. g. Christ Church, the most famous one	see Christ Church – a "must"
	the High Street – one of the world's great streets	wander along it
	student district in Cowley Road	enjoy nightlife at some good pubs and clubs
	the River Thames	go punting from Magdalen Bridge

	Carfax Tower	climb it to have a good view of the High Street from above
	Oxford Playhouse	go to – a performance of classical drama or comedy – a concert
Glastonbury	funky cafés, quirky shops, unusual events	– hang out for a while – enjoy the colourful ambience – maybe: feel the deep spiritual energies the area is supposed to have
	Glastonbury Tor	– go on a tour of it – learn about the myths and legends as regards its origins
	Glastonbury Abbey	– see its ruins, which are in 37 acres of parkland – supposed to be the resting place of King Arthur and Queen Guinevere
	Festivals: – the summer music festival – many lesser known festivals – the annual Majma dance festival in March	– enjoy Middle Eastern and North African dance and culture – attend dance performances, workshops, seminars – have delicious traditional food
Cardiff	Millennium Stadium	– watch a match – when there's a match on: feel the thrilling atmosphere in the city and in the stadium

Cardiff Bay	– go on a boat ride there from behind the Millennium Stadium – ultra modern – have a snack at a pavement café
Techniquest science museum at Mermaid Bay	– experience technique "live"/ "with your own hands"
Museum of Welsh Life	– visit the open air heritage museum in the grounds of St. Fagan's Castle, which goes back to the 16th century

2. **Hinweise:** *Sagen Sie in nicht mehr als jeweils zwei Sätzen, welche Art Stadt Oxford, Glastonbury und Cardiff sind, so lautet die Aufgabe. Lesen Sie alle drei Teiltexte nun noch einmal unter dem Blickwinkel Charakteristisches, Wesentliches, was diese drei Städte ausmacht. Markieren Sie alle Aussagen dazu. Hierbei ist es notwendig, auch zwischen den Zeilen zu lesen und notwendige Schlussfolgerungen zu ziehen. Beispiel: "Oxford – [...] It is dominated by 36 university colleges, [...].", d. h. ein wesentliches Charakteristikum der Stadt ist, dass sie eine Universitätsstadt ist. Vermerken Sie daher ggf. neben Ihren Markierungen auch kurze Verweise auf indirekt zum Ausdruck gebrachte wesentliche Merkmale der jeweiligen Stadt. Achten Sie auch auf Aussagen zur geografischen Lage der Orte, denn dies kann Einfluss auf den Charakter haben oder ganz einfach wichtig sein für den Leser.*

Schlüsseltextstellen:
Oxford: *Vermerk ggf.*
"Oxford is a town of culture and history." (l. 2)
"It is dominated by 36 university colleges, the most   *university town*
famous being Christ Church." (ll. 2/3)
"If you're looking for the nightlife, head across   *typical student*
Magdalen Bridge to Cowley Road. Here you will find   *life*
the student district, which has a number of good pubs
and clubs. Enjoy!" (ll. 6–8)
"Due to its proximity to London, Oxford is a popular
weekend break. It is strongly recommended that you stay
longer." (ll. 13/14)

Glastonbury:

"This <u>small market town</u> <u>in the county of Somerset</u> has <u>a</u>
<u>colourful ambience</u> and for many, this area is <u>consid-</u>
<u>ered to hold deep spiritual energies</u>. Funky cafés, <u>quirky</u>
shops, colourful people and <u>unusual</u> events mix together
to make Glastonbury <u>a great spot to hang out for a</u>
<u>while</u>." (ll. 17–20)

a town with
atmosphere

"Made <u>famous for its awesome summer music festival</u>,
there are also many lesser known festivals in Glastonbury. In March the town hosts the annual <u>Majma dance</u>
<u>festival</u>, a celebration of the best in Middle Eastern and
North African dance and culture [...]." (ll. 26–29)

many music and
dance festivals

Cardiff:

"Cardiff is <u>a delight</u> to visit <u>at any time of the year</u>,
whether there's a special event on or not." (ll. 33/34)

"In season, a cheap boat ride from behind the Millennium Stadium will take you to the <u>ultra modern Cardiff</u>
<u>Bay</u>." (ll. 37/38)

coastal town

"Enjoy exploring of this <u>vibrant Welsh town</u>, which is at
the same time <u>Europe's youngest capital city</u>."
(ll. 44/45)

Darstellungsform/Planung des Notierens:

*Als Darstellungsform wird Ihnen die Textform vorgegeben, wobei Sie nicht
mehr als zwei Sätze pro Stadt schreiben dürfen. Bei der Formulierung Ihrer
Sätze achten Sie darauf, dass Sie das wichtigste Charakteristikum an den
Anfang setzen.*

Oxford, near London, is a town of culture and history and a popular weekend
break destination for Londoners. It is also a university town with a typical
student life.

Glastonbury, a small market town in the county of Somerset, has a colourful
ambience and is a town with atmosphere. It is a great spot to hang out for a
while and to enjoy one of the many music and dance festivals there.

Cardiff, Europe's youngest capital city, is a Welsh coastal town and a vibrant
place worth visiting at any time of the year.

3. *Hinweise: Welchen dieser drei Ferienorte würden Sie bevorzugen? Begründen Sie Ihre Wahl. Bei dieser Aufgabe geht es nicht mehr um klassische Informationsverarbeitung, sondern um eine Umwälzung alles Erlesenen auf die eigene Person. Egal für welchen der drei Ferienorte Sie sich entscheiden, wichtig ist, dass Ihre Begründung möglichst textnah und schlüssig erfolgt. Zusätzliches Wissen, das Sie ggf. zu diesen drei Städten haben, ist irrelevant, kann aber knapp erwähnt werden.*

   Darstellungsform/Planung des Notierens:
   Als Darstellungsform wird Ihnen ein kurzer Text in zusammenhängender Form vorgegeben. Leiten Sie kurz ein, z. B. indem Sie sagen, dass sicherlich alle drei Orte interessant sind. Nennen Sie Ihren Favoriten und begründen Sie dann ausführlich, indem Sie darstellen, was für Sie besonders wichtig und reizvoll ist. Denken Sie auch an die den Aufgaben 1 bis 3 vorangestellte Situation: Ihre Gruppe plant eine Fahrt nach Großbritannien am Ende der Klasse 10. Ordnen Sie Ihre Gründe (First, Second, Moreover/Furthermore, Finally ...) und kündigen Sie ggf. Ihre Meinungsäußerung an (In my opinion/ To my mind/I think ...).

   Naturally, all three places have something to offer, from culture to history to atmosphere. But I would prefer to visit Oxford. There are several reasons for my choice. First, Oxford is near London and probably easy to reach from there. That might be important as our group is going to travel by plane. Second, in my opinion the town offers the greatest variety of cultural and other activities and there will be something for everyone to see and do. Moreover, Oxford is a famous English university town. We could experience student life there and enjoy the nightlife in the student district. Finally, the town of Oxford is simply a "must" for anyone who has never been to Great Britain before.

B Creative writing

1. *Hinweis: Aufgabe ist, ein Gespräch zu gestalten zwischen einem Jugendlichen und seinen Eltern/einem Elternteil. Gegenstand des Gespräches soll die Diskussion einer Reise sein, die der Jugendliche mit seinen Freunden geplant hat. Geben Sie der/dem Jugendlichen und den Freunden Namen. Vater und/oder Mutter reden Sie mit Mum/Dad an. Diskussion bedeutet nicht automatisch Streitgespräch, aber strittige Sachverhalte bieten sich natürlich an, z. B. Gefahren, Finanzielles, Vorurteile gegen einen Freund etc. Außerdem lässt sich ein strittiger Sachverhalt inhaltlich gut entwickeln und ausbauen. Reduzieren Sie das Gespräch auf Dinge wie Zeit, Ort, geplante Aktivitäten etc., könnte der Schreibgegenstand sehr schnell erschöpft sein. Steigen Sie einfach an einem beliebigen Punkt in das Gespräch ein. Erklärungen*

zur Situation sind nicht notwendig. Mit einer kurzen Aussage können Sie eine Situation herstellen, z. B. am Frühstückstisch "Thomas, could you pass me the coffee, please?" oder beim Fernsehen "Will you turn down the volume please?" oder im Auto "Be careful! There's something on the road!"
Stilistisch ist eine ungezwungene, z. T. auch jugendgemäße Umgangssprache anzustreben. Verwenden Sie Kurzformen. Sie sind für das Mündliche typisch. Beachten Sie beim Notieren, dass die unterschiedlichen Sprecherrollen auch als solche zu erkennen sind.

MUM: Thomas, could you pass me the coffee, please? By the way, I think we should talk about your trip to Lake Müritz again. Are you still thinking of going by moped?

THOMAS: Yeah. Where's the problem?

MUM: I talked to Daniel's mother the other day and she said she didn't think it was a good idea for you to go by moped.

THOMAS: She always fusses about things that are none of her business.

DAD: Thomas, don't be cheeky. I think she's right. I don't like it either. It's more than a hundred kilometres from here.

THOMAS: I thought we'd agreed that going there by train was much too expensive and too complicated with the tents and everything.

MUM: Yes, I know, but if you started on Saturday instead of Friday we could take you there in the car. Daniel's parents would fetch you the weekend after.

THOMAS: But how would we be able to get around when we're there? Walk, or hitchhike? I bet you won't like that either.

DAD: Thomas, try to be a bit more reasonable. There's a bus service all around Müritz National Park and with the Müritzcard you can use the ferries on the lake as well.

MUM: Dad's right. And apart from that you could rent a bike, couldn't you?

DAD: Anyway. Will you talk to Daniel and the others, please, and tell them what we suggest?

THOMAS: Hmm ...

DAD: Pardon?

THOMAS: Yes, alright.

MUM: Thomas, could you pass me the butter, please? By the way, Grandma rang up last night. If I were you, I'd call her back.

THOMAS: Do you think she'll give me some extra money?

MUM: Well, give it a try!

THOMAS: (Telephoning) Hi Grandma, this is Thomas. How's life? ...

2. *Hinweise: Sprachen können Brücken bauen, so lautet der Leitgedanke zur Aufgabe. Zeigen Sie, dass die Kenntnis von Fremdsprachen hilft, Menschen zu verbinden auf den unterschiedlichsten Ebenen. Sie können dabei Bezug nehmen auf Tourismus, Musik, die Arbeitswelt usw. Schreiben Sie einen Text von wenigstens 200 Wörtern. Beachten Sie aber, dass es sich dabei lediglich um eine Mindestwortzahl handelt.*

Diese Schreibaufgabe beinhaltet ein klassisches einsträngiges Erörterungsthema. Sie führen anhand ausgewählter Lebensbereiche den Nachweis, dass Fremdsprachen helfen die Menschen zu verbinden. Diese Aussage an sich ist einleuchtend und mit einem klaren „Ja" zu beantworten. Der Anspruch an die Bearbeitung ist jedoch nicht zu unterschätzen, da das Thema dazu verführt Klischees zu bedienen. Das trifft insbesondere für den Bereich Tourismus zu. Bemühen Sie sich hier um Differenzierung und vermeiden Sie Pauschalisierung. Cluburlaube und klassische Touristenreisen ermöglichen nicht wirklich den Brückenschlag mittels Sprache. Bestenfalls helfen sie Verständnis für fremde Kulturen zu entwickeln. Dagegen sind Schüleraustausche, Sprachreisen mit Familienunterbringung oder Individualreisen schon eher geeignet, Menschen miteinander zu verbinden. Der Vorschlag, den Nachweis anhand der Musik zu führen, ist etwas unglücklich gewählt. Hier erfolgt der Brückenschlag in der Regel vorrangig über die Melodie, weniger über die Liedtexte, Mehrsprachler einmal ausgenommen.

Gliedern Sie Ihren Text in bekannter Weise in Einleitung, Hauptteil und Schluss. Den Hauptteil ordnen Sie nach den zwei oder drei Lebensbereichen, zu denen Sie den Nachweis führen. Generell gilt, dass ein tiefgründiges Diskutieren einiger weniger Bereiche sachdienlicher ist als eine Häufung von Beispielen aus sehr vielen Bereichen. Verwenden Sie Vokabular des Ordnens (First/Let me begin ..., Second, Furthermore/Moreover, Finally). Wenn Sie eine sehr persönliche Meinung äußern, machen Sie dies deutlich (In my opinion/To my mind/I think/I believe). Große Sicherheit kann z. B. mit „I am sure" bekräftigt werden, Vagheit mit „I suppose/assume". Einleitung und Schluss nutzen Sie um den Leser zum Thema hinzuführen bzw. um die Kernaussagen Ihrer Diskussion noch einmal auf den Punkt zu bringen.

Languages can build bridges

Everyone knows the legendary joke about a German guest in an English restaurant. "Waiter, when will I become my steak?" And the waiter's dry reply: "I hope never, sir!" Even if the German guest made a serious mistake, he built a little bridge. The waiter will probably have told a lot of other people about the guest's funny question and they will have laughed about it time and again. In my text I will try to show that the knowledge of foreign languages helps to connect people in various areas of life.

2006-21

Let me begin with tourism. Nowadays for Germans travelling abroad on holiday does not necessarily mean that you can speak a foreign language. At popular holiday resorts and clubs all over the world German is spoken and you can book a package tour with a German-speaking guide to a lot of the classical tourist destinations. To my mind, this kind of tourism does not really build bridges. I believe that at best it helps to develop some understanding of foreign cultures and traditions.

But there are other forms, such as exchange visits, language tours and individual travelling, which may sometimes even be the starting point of a long-lasting friendship. Exchange visits between pupils of different nations are certainly a very good example of how languages can build bridges. The intensive private contact with ordinary people is the best way to get to know one another and to develop mutual understanding. Language tours with private accommodation are another good example, I am sure. Of course, all holidaymakers travelling on their own have good chance of building bridges that connect people. They simply need to have some knowledge of the country's language or of English as a lingua franca to make themselves understood. But naturally, it takes more than the command of a language to build ties with the native population. I believe it depends a lot on how far people use their language abilities to make friends with people of other nationalities.

Second, I will discuss music as a bridge-builder. Good music crosses borders and overcomes barriers. Melodies are understood without being translated. Thus, music is a good way to connect people of different backgrounds. Moreover, it helps to develop an understanding of foreign cultures and traditions. However, in my opinion it is not the language of the songs which has this power and influence but the melody. Therefore, I think that the example of music does not really work with regard to the saying that languages can build bridges.

Finally, I will write about the world of work. With the opening of the European market this saying could not be more true. Multilingualism has gained in importance and will see a further increase in significance in the near future, I am sure. More and more people work abroad regularly or for some time and need some knowledge in one or the other foreign language to tackle their jobs and everyday life away from home. They are often in close touch with their fellow workmates. They need to accept and respect one another because they have a joint goal. Building lasting bridges that really connect people begins when contacts go beyond people's work issues.

In conclusion, to say that languages can build bridges is certainly true for many spheres of life. However, it takes more than a good command of a language to connect people. Moreover, it is the contacts on the private level that have the best chance of becoming lasting ties.

Sicher durch das Abitur!

Klare Fakten, systematische Methoden, prägnante Beispiele sowie Übungsaufgaben auf Abiturniveau mit erklärenden Lösungen zur Selbstkontrolle.

Deutsch

Training Methoden Deutsch	Best.-Nr. 944062
Dramen analysieren und interpretieren	Best.-Nr. 944092
Erörtern und Sachtexte analysieren	Best.-Nr. 944094
Gedichte analysieren und interpretieren	Best.-Nr. 944091
Epische Texte analysieren und interpretieren	Best.-Nr. 944093
Abitur-Wissen Erörtern und Sachtexte analysieren	Best.-Nr. 944064
Abitur-Wissen Textinterpretation Lyrik, Drama, Epik	Best.-Nr. 944061
Abitur-Wissen Deutsche Literaturgeschichte	Best.-Nr. 94405
Abitur-Wissen Prüfungswissen Oberstufe	Best.-Nr. 94400
Kompakt-Wissen Rechtschreibung	Best.-Nr. 944065
Lexikon Autoren und Werke	Best.-Nr. 944081

Englisch

Übersetzungsübung	Best.-Nr. 82454
Grammatikübung	Best.-Nr. 82452
Themenwortschatz	Best.-Nr. 82451
Grundlagen der Textarbeit	Best.-Nr. 94464
Sprachmittlung	Best.-Nr. 94469
Textaufgaben Literarische Texte und Sachtexte	Best.-Nr. 94468
Grundfertigkeiten des Schreibens	Best.-Nr. 94466
Sprechfertigkeit mit CD	Best.-Nr. 94467
Abitur-Wissen Landeskunde Großbritannien	Best.-Nr. 94461
Abitur-Wissen Landeskunde USA	Best.-Nr. 94463
Abitur-Wissen Literaturgeschichte	Best.-Nr. 94465
Kompakt-Wissen Kurzgrammatik	Best.-Nr. 90461
Kompakt-Wissen Abitur Themenwortschatz	Best.-Nr. 90462

Französisch

Landeskunde Frankreich	Best.-Nr. 94501
Themenwortschatz	Best.-Nr. 94503
Literatur	Best.-Nr. 94502
Abitur-Wissen Literaturgeschichte	Best.-Nr. 94506
Kompakt-Wissen Kurzgrammatik	Best.-Nr. 945011
Kompakt-Wissen Abitur Themenwortschatz	Best.-Nr. 945010

Latein

Abitur-Wissen Lateinische Literaturgeschichte	Best.-Nr. 94602
Wiederholung Grammatik	Best.-Nr. 94601
Wortkunde	Best.-Nr. 94603
Kompakt-Wissen Kurzgrammatik	Best.-Nr. 906011

Pädagogik / Psychologie

Grundwissen Pädagogik	Best.-Nr. 92480
Grundwissen Psychologie	Best.-Nr. 92481

Religion

Katholische Religion 1 – gk	Best.-Nr. 84991
Katholische Religion 2 – gk	Best.-Nr. 84992
Abitur-Wissen gk ev. Religion Der Mensch zwischen Gott und Welt	Best.-Nr. 94973
Abitur-Wissen gk ev. Religion Die Verantwortung des Christen in der Welt	Best.-Nr. 94974
Abitur-Wissen Glaube und Naturwissenschaft	Best.-Nr. 94977
Abitur-Wissen Jesus Christus	Best.-Nr. 94978
Abitur-Wissen Die Frage nach dem Menschen	Best.-Nr. 94990
Abitur-Wissen Die Bibel	Best.-Nr. 94992
Abitur-Wissen Christliche Ethik	Best.-Nr. 94993
Lexikon Ethik und Religion	Best.-Nr. 94959

Ethik

Ethische Positionen in historischer Entwicklung – gk	Best.-Nr. 94951
Abitur-Wissen Philosophische Ethik	Best.-Nr. 94952
Abitur-Wissen Glück und Sinnerfüllung	Best.-Nr. 94953
Abitur-Wissen Freiheit und Determination	Best.-Nr. 94954
Abitur-Wissen Recht und Gerechtigkeit	Best.-Nr. 94955
Abitur-Wissen Religion und Weltanschauungen	Best.-Nr. 94956
Abitur-Wissen Wissenschaft – Technik – Verantwortung	Best.-Nr. 94957
Abitur-Wissen Politische Ethik	Best.-Nr. 94958
Lexikon Ethik und Religion	Best.-Nr. 94959

Kunst

Abitur-Wissen Kunst 1 Grundwissen Malerei	Best.-Nr. 94961
Abitur-Wissen Kunst 2 Analyse und Interpretation	Best.-Nr. 94962

Sport

Bewegungslehre – LK	Best.-Nr. 94981
Trainingslehre – LK	Best.-Nr. 94982

Wirtschaft/Recht

Betriebswirtschaft	Best.-Nr. 94851
Abitur-Wissen Volkswirtschaft	Best.-Nr. 94881
Abitur-Wissen Rechtslehre	Best.-Nr. 94882
Kompakt-Wissen Abitur Volkswirtschaft	Best.-Nr. 948501

Fachübergreifend

Tipps und Lernstrategien – Oberstufe	Best.-Nr. 10483
Referate und Facharbeiten – Oberstufe	Best.-Nr. 10484
Training Methoden Meinungen äußern, Ergebnisse präsentieren	Best.-Nr. 10486

(Bitte blättern Sie um)

Abitur-Prüfungsaufgaben

Von den Kultusministerien zentral gestellte Abitur-Prüfungsaufgaben, einschließlich des aktuellen Jahrgangs. Mit schülergerechten Lösungen.

Mathematik

Abiturprüfung Mathematik – LK Sachsen .... Best.-Nr. 145000
Abiturprüfung Mathematik – gk Sachsen .... Best.-Nr. 145100
Abiturprüfung Mathematik – LKN Sachsen-Anhalt .... Best.-Nr. 155000
Abiturprüfung Mathematik – GKN Sachsen-Anhalt .... Best.-Nr. 155100
Abiturprüfung Mathematik – LK Thüringen .... Best.-Nr. 165000
Abiturprüfung Mathematik – gk Thüringen .... Best.-Nr. 165100
Abiturprüfung Mathematik – LK Mecklenburg-Vorpommern .... Best.-Nr. 135000
Abiturprüfung Mathematik – gk Mecklenburg-Vorpommern .... Best.-Nr. 135100
Abiturprüfung Mathematik – gk/LK Brandenburg .... Best.-Nr. 125000

Deutsch

Abiturprüfung Deutsch – LK Sachsen .... Best.-Nr. 145400
Abiturprüfung Deutsch – gk Sachsen .... Best.-Nr. 145410
Abiturprüfung Deutsch – GKN/LKN Sachsen-Anhalt .... Best.-Nr. 155400
Abiturprüfung Deutsch – LK Thüringen .... Best.-Nr. 165400
Abiturprüfung Deutsch – gk Thüringen .... Best.-Nr. 165410
Abiturprüfung Deutsch – gk/LK Mecklenburg-Vorpommern .... Best.-Nr. 135410
Abiturprüfung Deutsch – gk/LK Brandenburg .... Best.-Nr. 125400

Englisch

Abiturprüfung Englisch – LK Sachsen .... Best.-Nr. 145460
Abiturprüfung Englisch – GKN/LKN Sachsen-Anhalt .... Best.-Nr. 155460
Abiturprüfung Englisch – gk/LK Thüringen .... Best.-Nr. 165460
Abiturprüfung Englisch – gk/LK Mecklenburg-Vorpommern .... Best.-Nr. 135460
Abiturprüfung Englisch – gk/LK Brandenburg .... Best.-Nr. 125460

Chemie

Abiturprüfung Chemie – gk/LK Sachsen .... Best.-Nr. 145730
Abiturprüfung Chemie – GKN/LKN Sachsen-Anhalt .... Best.-Nr. 155730
Abiturprüfung Chemie – gk/LK Thüringen .... Best.-Nr. 165730

Physik

Abiturprüfung Physik – LK Sachsen .... Best.-Nr. 145300
Abiturprüfung Physik – LKN Sachsen-Anhalt .. Best.-Nr. 155300
Abiturprüfung Physik – gk/LK Thüringen .... Best.-Nr. 165300
Abiturprüfung Physik – LK Mecklenburg-Vorpommern .... Best.-Nr. 135300

Biologie

Abiturprüfung Biologie – gk/LK Sachsen .... Best.-Nr. 145700
Abiturprüfung Biologie – LKN Sachsen-Anhalt Best.-Nr. 155700
Abiturprüfung Biologie – GKN Sachsen-Anhalt Best.-Nr. 155710
Abiturprüfung Biologie – LK Thüringen .... Best.-Nr. 165700
Abiturprüfung Biologie – gk Thüringen .... Best.-Nr. 165710
Abiturprüfung Biologie – LK Mecklenburg-Vorpommern .... Best.-Nr. 135700
Abiturprüfung Biologie – gk/LK Brandenburg .... Best.-Nr. 125700

Geschichte

Abiturprüfung Geschichte – LK Sachsen .... Best.-Nr. 145760
Abiturprüfung Geschichte – gk Sachsen .... Best.-Nr. 145780
Abiturprüfung Geschichte – LK Thüringen ..... Best.-Nr. 165760
Abiturprüfung Geschichte – gk/LK Brandenburg .... Best.-Nr. 125760

Geografie

Abiturprüfung Geografie – gk/LK Brandenburg .... Best.-Nr. 125900
Mündliche Abiturprüfung Geografie – gk Sachsen .... Best.-Nr. 145931

Wirtschaft/Recht

Abiturprüfung Wirtschaft/Recht – gk Thüringen .... Best.-Nr. 165880

Bestellungen bitte direkt an: STARK Verlagsgesellschaft mbH & Co. KG
Postfach 1852 · 85318 Freising · Tel: 08161 / 179-0 · FAX: 08161 / 179-51
Internet: www.stark-verlag.de · E-Mail: info@stark-verlag.de

Die echten Hilfen zum Lernen ...